TWAYNE'S WORLD AUTHORS SERIES

A Survey of the World's Literature

Sylvia E. Bowman, Indiana University

GENERAL EDITOR

GERMANY

Ulrich Weisstein, Indiana University

EDITOR

Georg Trakl

(TWAS 171)

TWAYNE'S WORLD AUTHORS SERIES (TWAS)

The purpose of TWAS is to survey the major writers —novelists, dramatists, historians, poets, philosophers, and critics—of the nations of the world. Among the national literatures covered are those of Australia, Canada, China, Eastern Europe, France, Germany, Greece, India, Italy, Japan, Latin America, New Zealand, Poland, Russia, Scandinavia, Spain, and the African nations, as well as Hebrew, Yiddish, and Latin Classical literatures. This survey is complemented by Twayne's United States Authors Series and English Authors Series.

The intent of each volume in these series is to present a critical-analytical study of the works of the writer; to include biographical and historical material that may be necessary for understanding, appreciation, and critical appraisal of the writer and to present all material in clear, concise English—but not to vitiate the scholarly content of the work by doing so.

Georg Trakl

By HERBERT LINDENBERGER
Stanford University

Twayne Publishers, Inc.   ::   New York

FOR EGON AND DOROTHEA SCHWARZ

Preface

This book is the product of a preoccupation with Trakl's poetry that goes back to the fall of 1952 when, as a Fulbright student at the University of Vienna, I attended a year-long series of lectures on Trakl given by Eugène Susini, a scholar then serving as cultural officer with the French embassy in Vienna. At a time when Trakl's name did not yet count for much in German literary histories, Susini presented a detailed, rigorous *explication de texte,* French-style, of every Trakl poem. Although I was never able to acclimate myself fully to the critical tradition within which Susini was working, my commitment to Trakl's poetry was so immediate and so strong that I quickly determined to write my doctoral dissertation—still owing on a comparative literature degree I was taking at the University of Washington—on Trakl. Once the degree was done with, I decided—wisely, I now see—never to prepare the dissertation for publication, though I subsequently developed several ideas contained in it in three papers I published on Trakl in the 1950's. For a number of years, while busy with projects on Wordsworth and Büchner, I wrote nothing on Trakl. Then, when I was asked to do this book, I quickly assented, expecting it to be a relatively simple task; it even occurred to me that I might salvage something from my dissertation. I turned out to be wrong: in the intervening years Trakl scholarship had changed radically, criticism in general had changed, and I had changed as well. Except for several lines on the metrics of "Helian," plus a few phrases and ideas I have used here and there, everything had to be thought out anew. The result was that I rediscovered Trakl.

In writing this book, I have attempted to fulfill two quite diverse aims—to provide an introduction to Trakl for serious readers of modern poetry and, at the same time, to make an original critical statement for scholars in the field of German literature. To achieve these aims I have had to come to terms with various problems, among them the nature of Trakl's development as a poet, his relation to the Symbolist tradition, the Christian element in his poetry, his peculiar methods of composition, and the manner in which he creates his own private mythology. Perhaps most fundamental of all, I have tried to demonstrate in precisely what ways a Trakl poem should be read. My major problem was how best to organize the book in order to accomplish these goals. Rather than disperse my efforts over too wide an area, I resolved to focus on a limited number of poems. The book thus consists of a detailed analysis of fifteen poems, each representing a different aspect of Trakl's art and development and each, as well, serving as the focal point for a discussion of one or two of the major problems that the critic of Trakl's poetry must inevitably face. For example, the section on "Helian" contains a discussion of Trakl's Christianity, while the section on the "Elis" poems deals largely with his private mythology.

In accordance with the format of this series, I have included short introductory and concluding chapters which sketch out the central facts about Trakl's life and his impact upon later poets and critics. I have provided my own translations for all the poems I discuss. These translations make no attempt to give anything more than a literal reading. Rhyme schemes for the rhymed poems are marked in columns to the right of my translations. Whenever a German word contains a secondary meaning which seems important for an understanding of the poem, I have indicated this secondary meaning in brackets. All fifteen poems are quoted both in German and English, except for the prose poem "Traum und Umnachtung," for which, because of its great length, I have omitted the German original. Quotations from Trakl's writings, to be cited simply by volume and page number within my text, refer to the two-volume critical edition, Georg Trakl, *Dichtungen und Briefe,* edited by Walther Killy and Hans Szklenar (Salzburg, 1969).

My most obvious acknowledgments are to Theodore Fiedler, Diana Hinze, Christiane Seiler, Günter Stoltz, Helena Szepe, and Sue Ellen Wright, who, as students in a seminar I gave on Trakl at Washington University, Saint Louis, in 1965, helped me to define many of the ideas contained in the book. More particularly, Mr. Fiedler's researches on the Trakl-Hölderlin relationship; Mrs. Seiler's on Trakl's influence on later poets; and Mrs. Hinze's and Mrs. Szepe's on the history of Trakl's reputation, have all—as they will be the first to recognize—left their traces in my work.

In addition, I wish to express my gratitude to my former

Preface

colleague Ada Haussmann Schmidt, whose many discerning suggestions for revision I was almost never able to turn down; to my former colleague Egon Schwarz and my wife, Claire F. Lindenberger, for a critical reading of the manuscript; to the University of California, Riverside, and Washington and Stanford Universities, for financing the project in its various stages; and to the following publishers for permission to quote: Otto Müller Verlag, Salzburg, for permission to quote the poems I discuss from the critical edition; Wesleyan University Press and Longman Group Ltd. for permission to quote James Wright's "Rain," from *The Branch Will Not Break* (Copyright 1962 by James Wright); and Deutsche Verlagsanstalt, Stuttgart, for permission to quote Paul Celan's "Die Jahre von Dir zu Mir," from *Mohn und Gedächtnis*. An earlier version of the section on "Traum und Umnachtung" was printed in *Festschrift für Bernhard Blume* (Göttingen, 1967). I have, in addition, lifted a few sentences and ideas from my three earlier articles on Trakl listed in the bibliography.

Stanford, California   HERBERT LINDENBERGER

Contents

Contents

Chronology

1887   Born in Salzburg, Austria, the fifth of seven children of a successful hardware dealer.

1891   Birth of his sister Grete.

1892   Enrolls in a Catholic elementary school, but receives his religious training in a Protestant school, where he meets his lifelong friend Erhard Buschbeck.

1897   Enters the Salzburg *Staatsgymnasium*.

1901   Is forced to repeat the fourth grade in the *Gymnasium*.

1904   Active for the next two years in a Salzburg literary coterie which was first called "Apollo," then "Minerva."

1905   Fails to be promoted from the seventh grade in the *Gymnasium*. Begins a three-year apprenticeship in a Salzburg pharmacy. Associates with Gustav Streicher, a local *poète maudit*.

1906   Two one-act plays, both of them failures, performed on separate occasions at the Salzburg municipal theater. First publication of a literary work—a piece of impressionistic prose—in a Salzburg newspaper.

1908   First publication of a poem in the same newspaper. Successfully completes his apprenticeship. Enrolls in the University of Vienna for a two-year training course in pharmacy.

1909   Prepares his first collection of poems, for which he is unable to find a publisher. With the help of the critic Hermann Bahr publishes three poems in the *Neue Wiener Journal*, his first publication outside Salzburg.

1910   Death of his father. Completes his university training. Begins his one-year service in the Austro-Hungarian army, is stationed in Vienna. Associates with members of an avant-garde-oriented group in Vienna.

1911   After military service works briefly in a Salzburg pharmacy. Associates with another Salzburg *poète maudit*, Karl Hauer.

1912   Returns to army service, is sent to work in the pharmacy of a military hospital in Innsbruck. Establishes close friendship with Ludwig von Ficker, editor of the Innsbruck literary-philosophical journal *Der Brenner*, in which Trakl publishes his poetry regularly for the remainder of his life. Leaves active service; briefly holds a government job in Vienna.

1913   Wanders between Vienna, Salzburg, and Innsbruck while desperately seeking out new career opportunities. Briefly holds another government post in Vienna. Becomes acquainted with Karl Kraus and Adolf Loos, with whom he vacations in Venice. Publishes his first volume of poems, *Gedichte*.

1914   Visits his sister Grete while she is ill in Berlin, where he meets the poetess Else Lasker-Schüler. Second volume of poems, *Sebastian im Traum*, accepted for publication. Through Ficker's mediation, receives a substantial financial gift anonymously from the philosopher Ludwig Wittgenstein. Reenters military service during mobilization and is sent to the eastern front, where he takes care of wounded soldiers. Suffers mental breakdown; spends a month in a Cracow hospital, where he dies of a self-inflicted overdose of cocaine.

CHAPTER 1

Trakl as Poète Maudit

A S modern poets go, Georg **Trakl** is a rather unsatisfactory subject for biography. He was, first of all, the total antithesis of the man of letters. Unlike his contemporary Rilke, who kept in touch with the literary worlds of Germany and France (not to mention the aristocratic connections he so assiduously cultivated), Trakl had little contact with contemporary movements and personalities. Among men of his own stature he knew only Oscar Kokoschka, the painter; Karl Kraus, the satirist; and Kraus's friend Adolf Loos, one of the pioneers of modern architecture. With the possible exception of the German poetess Else Lasker-Schüler, Trakl never so much as met a poet who can be named in the same breath with him.

Moreover, despite the fact that a few persons who knew him are still alive, the amount of information on him which is both dependable and relevant is pitifully scarce. One can, in fact, point to weeks and even months during the major period of his writing when next to nothing is known of him. He left no diary, and the 145 letters that remain are not only short, but they tell us little except that he lived in an almost constant state of suffering, was always short of funds, and took great pains to revise his poems. Other letters which might have told us more—for instance, those he wrote to his sister Grete—have never turned up. Accounts written about him by his friends are all too often colored by their sense of awe toward him; those given out by surviving members of his family to visiting scholars and journalists have, in turn, been colored by a fanatic desire to portray the family in the most respectable possible light. Moreover, serious scholarly investigation of his life and work was so long delayed that by the time it got started—in the late 1950's—a number of important documents had disappeared as a result of World War II.

All this is not to say that Trakl's life, even what we know of it, was in itself uninteresting. It has already served as the subject for at least two fictionalized biographies,[1] and a Swiss psychiatrist, Theodor Spoerri, has managed to fill a slim volume with clinical interpretations of his mind and art.[2] The various deviations from the bourgeois norm which are known to have marked his life—incest, addiction to alcohol and drugs, suicide, not to speak of his total inability to hold a job for any length of time—have given Trakl a degree of notoriety among people not otherwise interested in poetry. He is much more the sort of figure out of whom myths—both of a serious and a frivolous kind—can be constructed than the sort who provides material for scholarly biography. Although our knowledge of his life is notably lacking in detail, the patterns which give it shape seem familiar enough to anyone acquainted with the biographies of modern authors. For Trakl is an almost pure example of that genus of poets which Verlaine, in his study of writers such as Baude-laire, Rimbaud, and Verlaine himself, labeled the *poètes maudits*. Given the fact that Trakl's poetry was deeply influenced by the work of these three major French poets, one is led to suspect that the relationship between a writer's life style and his poetic style may be something more than a coincidence.

As with most of the great *poètes maudits* before him, Trakl's background was impeccably middle class; or at least that was the way it must have looked to his home town. His father, Tobias Trakl, was the proprietor of a prosperous and highly respected hardware business in Salzburg; he was patriarchal, good-natured, devoted to his work, and had little discernible influence on his son.[3] The Trakl family background reflects the variegated ethnic patterns and movements typical of the Austro-Hungarian Empire. Tobias' ancestors were Germans who had moved from Swabia to Hungary many generations before. Tobias was born in Sopron, Hungary, later moved to Wiener Neustadt, an indus-trial town in lower Austria near Vienna, and finally settled in Salzburg. In the course of these moves, the spelling of his name changed from Trackel to Trackl and finally to Trakl. Georg's mother, Maria Halik Trakl, of partly Czech origin, was born in Wiener Neustadt, where she met her husband.

In two important respects, however, the family was not typical. First, since Tobias was of long-standing Protestant background (his wife left the Catholic church at the time of their marriage), the children were raised as Protestants within an overwhelm-ingly Catholic culture. Second, Maria Trakl not only divorced her first husband to marry Tobias but bore the latter a child

some three months before she could marry him. The decision
to move to Salzburg, one assumes, was caused by what, in its
time and place, must have been considered a most questionable
marriage. It is unknown to what extent, if any, the Trakl children were aware of the circumstances surrounding the marriage.

Maria Trakl was reserved by nature, suffered from depres-
sions, took opium, and saw relatively little of her children. Georg,
born February 3, 1887, and the fourth of her six children who
survived to adulthood, was later to express strongly hostile feelings toward her. She was interested principally in music and
antiques and, during her periods of depression, would retire
to her room for days on end. Her husband, whose first wife had
died, was fifteen years her senior and had brought a son, Wilhelm, from his first marriage into the family.

The Trakls enjoyed the comforts and professed the attitudes
typical of the middle class of their time. They lived in a large
house near Tobias' store, had an ample supply of servants, and
saw to it that their children were early exposed to what passed
for culture. The children's French governess, Marie Boring, who
probably exerted a greater influence on them than did the mother,
trained them to speak French among themselves. The children
were given piano lessons and were taken to concerts at the
Mozarteum and to dramatic performances at the city's repertory
theater. Although Georg found the family atmosphere thoroughly
repressive, it is evident from his poetry that he was able to
respond to certain aspects of his childhood environment, above
all the household garden, the nearby Baroque churches and
palaces, and the forested hills that surround the city.

Among all the members of his family, Georg's sister, Grete,
who was five years his junior, was the one to whom he felt the
closest ties. She grew up under his influence, looked strikingly
like him, and remained as emotionally unstable as her brother
throughout her short life, which, like his, ended in suicide. The
psychiatrist Spoerri, who investigated the family background
long after both brother and sister were dead, claims to have
unmistakable evidence of a sexual relationship between the
two, but was unable to divulge his sources in print.[4] Even without Spoerri's investigation, the reader of Georg's poetry, in which
incest figures as a theme and in which the sister serves as a
central, obsessive image, is likely to assume the existence of
an incestuous relationship.

Little is known about Georg's early childhood. Members of his family claim that he was a relatively "normal" child, and several of his friends have testified that it was not until early adolescence that he showed much evidence of the instability which was increasingly to dominate his life. Trakl, on the other hand, later told friends that when he was two his family took him to be an imbecile.

His formal schooling began in 1892. Although he was sent to a Catholic school, he was released for two afternoons a week to take religious instruction from a local Protestant pastor. In 1897, when he was ten, he entered the so-called humanistic secondary school, which in the German-speaking countries in his time consisted of an eight-year program with heavy stress on Greek and Latin, and whose grotesquely authoritarian atmosphere has become legendary through such works as Frank Wedekind's *Frühlings Erwachen* (*Spring's Awakening*) and Heinrich Mann's *Professor Unrat* (*The Blue Angel*). It is none too surprising that a sensitive child like Georg was unable to survive this atmosphere. By his fourth year he had failed Latin, Greek, and mathematics and was forced to repeat the year's work; at the end of the seventh year, he failed in these subjects once again and dropped out of school altogether.

During his school years, Trakl displayed his reaction to the educational system in various ways. Although he maintained a high degree of reserve, he also took to acting strangely in dress and manner. His fellow students, moreover, noted a brooding, sometimes even defiant quality behind his outwardly passive stance. In early adolescence he was introduced to narcotics by a pharmacist's son, and by the end of his school career he was known to carry a bottle of chloroform around with him regularly and to dip his cigarettes in an opium solution. At one time his family was shocked to find him stretched out on the sofa in a narcotic state; at another he was found lying unconscious on a Salzburg hillside in winter. During this period he also began to frequent brothels regularly.

Trakl's interest in literature came not so much from his official schooling—his best grades were in physical education—as from his private reading and his participation in the literary activities of adolescents his own age. Between 1904 and 1906 he was a member of a writers' club, which at first called itself Apollo but later changed its name to Minerva. There was nothing unique about such groups in the German-speaking countries at that time. The various members of these groups met in cafés, where they read their poetry aloud to one another. They cultivated whatever seemed appropriately avant-garde at the moment and lost no opportunity to assert their independence from the bourgeois world of their families. One might add that nearly all of Trakl's young literary friends eventually abandoned literature for professions none too different in kind from those of their fathers. But it is also significant that through his membership in such literary groups Trakl felt motivated to write regularly and was introduced to some of the more vital literary and philosophical forces—both German and foreign—of his day. Even before 1904 Trakl and several friends had taken up Nietzsche and Dostoevsky; and the latter continued to influence him profoundly throughout his poetic career. With his Apollo and Minerva friends he read and imitated Baudelaire, Verlaine, and Maeterlinck, among the recent French poets, and George and Hofmannsthal among the German poets who had come to prominence during the preceding decade. Trakl is supposed to have been the most productive writer in the group, and much of his writing consisted of prose sketches. The small amount of work from this period that remains extant today is not only derivative, as one would expect, but also seems singularly lacking in promise.

In September, 1905, after it had become evident that Trakl could not complete secondary school, he became an apprentice in one of Salzburg's older pharmacies, the White Angel. After a three-year apprenticeship he would be eligible to undertake a two-year course at the University of Vienna, as a result of which he could be licensed as a pharmacist. Carl Hinterhuber, the proprietor of the White Angel, had little faith in his apprentice's talents as a pharmacist, but Trakl is known to have worked conscientiously at his job. Whatever other attractions the field of pharmacy may have had for him, there can be no doubt that he felt tempted by the easy accessibility of all manner of narcotics. During his three years of apprenticeship his style of living became increasingly different from the style in which he had been reared. He wore his hair long, cultivated somewhat dandified clothes, and used every available opportunity to indicate his defiance of middle-class life. In the brothel he frequented he sometimes sat for hours drinking wine and de-

livering monologues before an aging prostitute. Moreover, the
emotional patterns which were to dominate his final years had
already become evident now. Moments of joyful exuberance
would regularly alternate with periods of self-contained silence
and depression; suicide threats became frequent.

During his apprenticeship in the pharmacy, Trakl gradually
came to be locally known as a writer. Beginning in 1906 he
published occasional impressionistic prose sketches and book
reviews in Salzburg newspapers. And in the course of this year
he had the good fortune to have two one-act plays performed
in the local theater. The first of these, *Totentag* (*All Souls Day*),
received mixed notices, but the second, *Fata Morgana*, was
judged a total failure in the newspapers, and as a result Trakl
destroyed all copies of both plays. What little is known about
these plays can only be reconstructed from the newspaper reviews (reprinted in II, 511-17). The pieces contained motifs
such as self-deception and jealousy, and *Totentag*, significantly,
had a heroine named Grete, who, as far as one can tell from the
reviews, seems to have had close ties with her clairvoyant blind
brother. The reviewers mention the influence of Ibsen, Nietzsche,
Hofmannsthal and Maeterlinck, but Trakl probably absorbed
these influences by way of a local, now totally forgotten, play-
wright named Gustav Streicher, about whom he wrote one of his
few printed pieces of critical prose (I, 207-8). Trakl's senior by
fourteen years, Streicher had befriended and encouraged the
young poet, who, in turn, was doubtlessly attracted by the older
man's status in Salzburg as a "loose-living" Bohemian and out-
cast. It was Streicher who, through his contacts with the Salzburg
theater, made possible the production of Trakl's plays. Although
his disillusionment with the reception of *Fata Morgana* pre-
vented him from ever again establishing an active relationship
with any theater, Trakl made at least three subsequent attempts
within dramatic form—a full-length verse tragedy, *Don Juans
Tod* (*Don Juan's Death*), written about 1906-8 and of which
he destroyed everything but small fragments; a short verse play
for puppets, *Blaubart* (*Bluebeard*), written in 1910; and an
untitled fragment of a prose play written in 1914.

In the fall of 1908, Trakl left for Vienna to begin his two-year
training course at the university. He took badly to the anonymity
of life in a big city and moved frequently from one lonely fur-
nished room to another. During these years, however, he was

able not only to complete his course satisfactorily but also to produce a goodly amount of poetry, little of which, however, seems sufficiently mature today to enhance his reputation. Trakl was spared total isolation through the fact that a number of his Salzburg friends were studying in Vienna at the same time. His closest contact was with Erhard Buschbeck, a fellow Protestant from Salzburg, whom he had known since the mid-1890's. Buschbeck, who arrived in Vienna a year after Trakl, had a notable talent for quickly discerning what was significant in the latest developments in the various arts and for getting to know those who wielded power in the artistic world. Vienna at this time was experiencing considerable ferment in the arts, for this was the period in which Schönberg and his disciples, as well as figures such as Loos and Kokoschka, were working to subvert the principles upon which their respective art forms had traditionally been based. Kokoschka was even working in two forms, painting and drama, at the time. Since Trakl was too shy and unworldly to look up anybody on his own, what little he experienced of this ferment came through his friendship with Buschbeck, who constantly prodded him to make his presence felt in literary circles. It was through Buschbeck, for instance, that Trakl met the eminent older critic and literary arbiter, Hermann Bahr, who arranged for the publication, in 1909, of three Trakl poems in a prominent Viennese newspaper, the *Neue Wiener Journal* (*New Viennese Journal*). Buschbeck later published some Trakl poems in an avant-garde publication, *Der Ruf* (*The Call*), which he helped edit; and, from 1909 onward, he worked unsuccessfully to get a collection of his friend's poems published in book form (this early collection, entitled *Aus goldenem Kelch* [*Out of a Golden Chalice*], and consisting of what, in retrospect, seem very immature poems, was finally published in 1939 under Buschbeck's editorship). Through Buschbeck, Trakl later became a member of a so-called Academic Association for Literature and Music, a group of avant-garde-oriented students which Buschbeck headed. Yet Trakl's life in Vienna remained essentially lonely, and there is no evidence that his few contacts with fellow writers had any major effect on his own artistic development.

Shortly before Trakl completed his pharmacy degree in the summer of 1910 his father died, and although his mother and half-brother continued to run the family business until 1913,

Trakl was no longer able to count on sufficient financial help from home to meet his need for alcohol and drugs. His finances were so bad at one point that he was even forced to sell his set of Dostoevsky's works.

As soon as the degree was finished, he was conscripted into the Austrian army for a one-year term of duty. In Trakl's day the term was ordinarily three years, but by virtue of his middle-class status and education he was allowed to opt for the shorter term. Trakl's stay in the army was not as unpleasant an experience for him as one might expect: he was given a job in Vienna in the medical corps and was not even required to live in barracks. Military service, one suspects, became for him a way of delaying the start of a career and thus of avoiding the day-to-day decisions that would be necessary once he was out on his own.

After he had completed his service in late 1911, Trakl's life was to consist of a constant shifting between various jobs in Vienna, Salzburg, and Innsbruck. The first few months after leaving the army were spent in Salzburg, where he took a position in the pharmacy in which he had served his apprentice-ship. Now that he had to start an active career, he virtually broke down. He felt himself so emotionally oppressed, for instance, by the task of waiting on customers that in the course of one morning he is said to have sweated through six shirts. He lasted less than two months on the job. During this time he formed a close attachment to an older man, Karl Hauer, who, like Streicher before him, served as a drinking companion and fellow rebel. But Hauer, who collaborated with Karl Kraus on the latter's iconoclastic journal, *Die Fackel* (*The Torch*), was an intellectual of greater substance than Streicher and had an anarchistically oriented social and political philosophy of his own which may, to some degree, have rubbed off on his younger friend.

Because he was unable to keep his job in the pharmacy, Trakl applied for reenlistment in the army and, in April, 1912, was assigned to a post in the pharmacy of an army hospital in Innsbruck. Although this job lasted little more than half a year, Trakl's move to Innsbruck turned out to be the most fortunate step he had ever taken, for it brought him together with a circle of intellectuals who recognized and nurtured his talent, saw

to it that his poems were published, and, even more important
for Trakl himself, were always on hand to give him comfort
and shelter. This circle was centered around a semimonthly
journal, *Der Brenner* (named after the nearby mountain pass),
whose editor, Ludwig von Ficker, a kindly, deeply religious
man seven years his senior, was to play the dual roles of parent
and intellectual guide for the remaining two and a half years
of Trakl's life.

From their isolated Alpine bastion, Ficker and his circle stood
for earnestness and integrity against what they took to be the
decadence and triviality of the fashionable views emanating from
Vienna. The intellectual orientation of *Der Brenner*, which
pioneered in the revival of Kierkegaard, could be described as
a kind of Christian existentialism. It was greatly respected by
avant-garde circles in Vienna, especially by Karl Kraus, who
referred to it as the only "honest" periodical in Austria. Shortly
before Trakl became personally acquainted with Ficker and his
friends, the journal had published its first Trakl poem. Characteristically, the poem had not been submitted by Trakl himself
but by one of Erhard Buschbeck's literary associates in Vienna.
From late 1912 until Trakl's death, every issue of *Der Brenner*
contained at least one, sometimes several, Trakl poems. Although
Trakl had produced a number of fine poems between 1909 and
1912, it is significant that nearly all the poems on which his
reputation as a major poet is based were written after he had
become intimate with the *Brenner* circle.

In November, 1912, apparently as a result of a fight with an
officer who had reprimanded him for spitting on the floor, Trakl
asked for and was granted permission to change from active
to reserve status in the army. At precisely this time his poetry
was undergoing a major stylistic change through the impact
that a German translation of Rimbaud's works had recently
made on him. This change consisted of a shift from rhymed to
free verse and, even more centrally, of a growth in verbal complexity, which, in turn, made possible a vastly greater thematic
scope. During December, 1912, and January, 1913, he wrote
"Helian," his most ambitious poem to date and the first major
product of this artistic breakthrough. At the same time, he made
halfhearted attempts to establish himself in a financially secure
position. He was granted a clerical position in the labor ministry

in Vienna but delayed starting the job for several weeks while
working on his poem in Salzburg and Innsbruck. When he
finally arrived in Vienna in late December, he quit after having
been on the job only two hours. Feeling that he could not work
on his poem in Vienna, he returned to Innsbruck, where he
finished it while living in Ficker's house, which was pictur-
esquely located in the outskirts of the city at the base of towering
peaks. Ficker and other members of the *Brenner* group, notably
Karl Borromäus Heinrich, who soon after wrote the first important critical assessment of Trakl's work, immediately recognized "Helian" as one of the central achievements in the history
of German verse.

Trakl spent the remainder of the winter in Salzburg, for he
felt he should be on hand while his mother and step-brother
were closing out the family firm. Then, in April, he returned
to Innsbruck, where he took up offers of hospitality from Ficker
as well as from Ficker's brother, who lived in a manor outside
the city. During the preceding months, Buschbeck had made
another unsuccessful attempt to find a publisher for a selection
of Trakl's poems. In April, shortly after this rejection, Trakl
received a letter from Kurt Wolff, an enterprising young Leipzig publisher, who offered to print a volume of his work. Wolff
had come across Trakl's poems in the pages of *Der Brenner* and
immediately recognized their worth. About the same time, in
fact, he had discovered and published the early writings of
Franz Kafka, and during the coming years he was to emerge
as the leading publisher of the Expressionist generation. Without consulting Trakl, Wolff's firm decided to do a small selection
of his verse in a series (*"Der jüngste Tag,"* the same series that
first printed Kafka's *Verwandlung* [*Metamorphosis*]) before at-
tempting a larger volume, and Trakl, disappointed that the
larger volume would not be published immediately, sent an
angry telegram, drafted by Ficker, which threatened to break
off negotiations. The firm, surprised at the demands being made
by an unknown writer, suggested a compromise, and the collection, under the unassuming title *Gedichte* (*Poems*), appeared in
July of the same year.

During 1913 and early 1914 Trakl still made occasional attempts to build a more stable existence for himself. He sent
out inquiries for positions as pharmacist in such diverse locations

as the Vienna General Hospital, the newly created nation of
Albania, and the Dutch East Indies. But the only job he was
ever to hold again, except for his war service, was a minor civil
service post in the war ministry in Vienna, which he quit after
less than a month in the summer of 1913. While in Vienna that
summer he became closely acquainted with Kraus and Loos,
whom he joined, together with Ficker and the writer Peter
Altenberg, for a two-week holiday in Venice in August. Except
for a short trip to Lake Garda with Ficker the next spring,
this was to be Trakl's only stay outside the German-speaking
countries. His letters to Ficker from Vienna during the succeeding months reveal what seems a greater degree of despera-
tion than those of any other period. Yet these months, as well
as the first few months of 1914, when he was back in Innsbruck,
were artistically the most productive of his life. His poetry,
which shows the impact of Hölderlin during this period, was
now entering its most elaborate phase, a phase, moreover, in
which he experimented with the prose poem, returned briefly
to rhymed forms, and developed his free verse into an instrument of even greater complexity than it had been at the time
of the composition of "Helian."

Trakl returned to Innsbruck in December, 1913, and that
month gave a public reading—the only one he was ever to give—
of his work under the sponsorship of *Der Brenner*. At this time
he began the preparation of his second volume of poems, *Sebastian im Traum* (*Sebastian Dreaming*), which Wolff hoped to
publish in 1914, but which, because of the war, was delayed
until after Trakl's death.

In March, 1914, Trakl rushed to Berlin to the bedside of his
sister Grete, who was gravely ill from the effects of a miscar-
riage. Since their childhood, Trakl had had little contact with
Grete except during the academic year 1909-10, when they
were both studying in Vienna. Grete, who was an accomplished
pianist, had gone to Berlin in 1910 to study with the composer-
pianist Ernst von Dohnanyi and two years later had married
Arthur Langen, a bookseller considerably her senior. The marriage was an unhappy one. Grete's life had become as unstable
as that of her brother, and, like him—apparently even as a
result of his influence on her—she had become addicted to drugs.
The Langens belonged to Berlin's literary Bohemia, and as a

consequence Trakl, during his ten-day visit to his sister, was able to meet such personalities as Herwarth Walden, editor of the avant-garde journal *Der Sturm,* and the poetess Else Lasker-Schüler, Walden's former wife, with whom Trakl struck up an immediate friendship. Although Grete recovered from her illness, she survived her brother by less than three years. After trying unsuccessfully to rid herself of the drug habit, she shot herself in 1917 while attending a party.

The relatively few accounts we have of Trakl's appearance, conversation, and personality come largely from his last two years, the period of his association with the *Brenner* group. By appearance he was muscular, blondish, above middle height, with somewhat slanted eyes. Observers frequently mentioned the sharp juxtaposition of opposing qualities in his manner. For example, a Swiss writer, Hans Limbach, who met Trakl briefly while visiting the *Brenner* group early in 1914, reports an "uncommonly dignified" quality in the poet's appearance, yet notes directly after this that "a dark, almost evil feature gave him [Trakl] a criminal-like fascination."[5] Moments of saintliness often alternated with moments of brutality. In a similarly alternating way an extreme self-enclosedness would give way to a compulsive sort of openness. Thus Kokoschka, who described Trakl as a "fellow apostate against middle-class life,"[6] reports that he would sit silently for long periods on a beer keg in Kokoschka's Vienna studio, then start a seemingly endless monologue, and finally fall silent again. As recorded by his friends, his conversation had a persistently cryptic and prophetic quality. "That is our Lord Christ," he once said pointing to a calf's head exhibited as a prize at a peasant fair.[7] His talk, like his poetry, also showed a fascination with death. The poet Theodor Däubler reports him as speaking constantly of death while on a walk through the countryside in the spring of 1914. "We fall into an inapprehensible blackness," Trakl told Däubler. "How could dying, the moment which leads into eternity, ever be short?"[8]

The obsession with death which culminated in Trakl's suicide increased during his final months through his participation in World War I. If the war had not come, Trakl, whatever his emotional condition, would at least have had a measure of financial security for the next few years, for in July, 1914, he (as well as Rilke) received a sizable gift from an anonymous donor.

The donor turned out to be the young and still unknown philosopher, Ludwig Wittgenstein, who had decided to give away his inheritance to worthy poets and artists and had called on Ficker to choose the beneficiaries and disburse the money. By the time Trakl received his gift, however, the mobilization had begun, and he was called back to active service as a medical officer with the rank of lieutenant. About this time he handed Ficker the following note, which may not only serve as a statement of his poetics but which also, through its allusions to death, despair, compassion, guilt, repentance, and the writing of poetry, pulls together many of the diverse strands out of which his life was woven:

Gefühl in den Augenblicken totenähnlichen Seins: Alle Menschen sind der Liebe wert. Erwachend fühlst du die Bitternis der Welt; darin ist alle deine ungelöste Schuld; dein Gedicht eine unvollkommene Sühne.

Feeling in the moments of deathlike existence: All human beings are worthy of love. Waking, you feel the world's bitterness; in this lies all your unresolved [unredeemed] guilt; your poem an incomplete atonement.   (I, 463)

In late August, Trakl joined a detachment from Innsbruck and was sent to the province of Galicia in Austrian-occupied Poland. During the following weeks, the swiftly advancing Russians inflicted one defeat after another on the poorly led Austrian army, which retreated in a state of great confusion. According to a recently discovered medical report (*see* II, 729-30), Trakl showed serious mental symptoms as soon as he left Innsbruck. At one point, after trying to rush into battle, he had to be disarmed by six men. Yet his early letters from the front show no evidence of emotional breakdown and, in fact, are mainly concerned with the reception of *Sebastian im Traum,* which he thought, mistakenly, had already appeared. A physician even reports him in a fine mood when they met at an inn, where Trakl, who had not wanted to live in the hospital to which he had been assigned, had rented a room. When the physician asked him what was worth reading in modern poetry, Trakl immediately started speaking of Verlaine and Rimbaud.

But in late October he wrote Ficker from an army hospital in Cracow that he was under observation for severe depression.

Ficker rushed to Cracow, where Trakl told him that during the Battle of Grodek over a month earlier he had been placed in charge of ninety badly wounded men who were being housed in a barn. Since there were no doctors on hand, he had taken care of the men by himself for two days. At one point he heard a gun go off, and when he looked around, he saw that one of the men had shot himself in the head; parts of his brain, Trakl reported, were sticking to the wall. Unable to bear the sight, Trakl walked outside, only to notice that a number of corpses were dangling from a row of bare trees on the local square; the hanged men, it turned out, were members of the local population whom the Austrian authorities had suspected of disloyalty. Soon after, while having dinner with his fellow officers, Trakl suddenly declared he could go on no longer and would have to shoot himself. He rushed out but was disarmed before he could pull the trigger. Then he was sent to the hospital, which, according to the report sent to Trakl's family after his death, was treating him for dementia praecox, a term which at that time could include a wide variety of mental disturbances.

Ficker, who has left a detailed and moving account of his visit to the hospital, found Trakl reading the poems of Johann Christian Günther, a talented *poète maudit* of two centuries before, with whom Trakl felt obvious affinities. Trakl declared Günther's poems to be the "bitterest which any German poet ever wrote" and reminded Ficker that Günther had died at twenty-seven, which was exactly Trakl's age.[9] Trakl read aloud to Ficker not only from Günther's work, but he also recited his own two most recent poems, "Klage" ("Lament") and "Grodek," which he had written at the front. At one point during Ficker's visit, Trakl expressed the fear that he would be court-martialed and executed for his conduct after the battle. The day after Ficker left, Trakl sent him two letters, one containing revisions of two poems he had written several years before, the other a copy of "Klage" and "Grodek," plus a request that his sister Grete inherit his money and his possessions. Less than a week later, Trakl took an overdose of cocaine, which he had managed to keep hidden from the hospital authorities. For a day he remained in a coma. He died on November 3. A few days before, Trakl had written to Wittgenstein, then also on the eastern front, asking his donor, whom he had never met, to visit him in the hospital. By the time Wittgenstein arrived, Trakl had been dead for three days. He was buried in Cracow, but in 1925 his bones were moved to Innsbruck, where, after a ceremony attended by his friends, he was buried in a cemetery near Ficker's home.

CHAPTER 2

Toward the Objective Image: Poems Through 1912

I "Die drei Teiche in Hellbrunn" and Other Early Poems

ALTHOUGH Trakl had been writing poems since adolescence, it was not until mid-1909, when he was twenty-two, that he produced any which an anthologist of German poetry would be likely to include in a selection of his work. Even a quick reading of Trakl's earlier poems gives the impression of warmed-over versions of works by the more respected writers of the period. The marks of Rimbaud, Hölderlin, and Dostoevsky, the three major formative influences on Trakl's mature work, can already be found in these early poems, although at this point their influence was quite undigested. Nietzsche's most famous lyric, "Das tiefe Lied" ("The Profound Song"), was imitated by Trakl in a poem (I, 228) which is the more ludicrous the more closely it follows its model. One of Baudelaire's city poems, "A une passante" ("To a Woman Passing By"), was transformed into a sentimental poem (I, 255) that totally lacks the concreteness and control of the original. Hofmannsthal, Verlaine, and Maeterlinck not only contributed a number of themes and images, but in Trakl's hands their intense lyricism often turned into a facile and vague mellifluousness.[1]

Since nearly all of Trakl's extant early poems belong to the group he gave to his friend Buschbeck in mid- or late 1909 in the hope of finding a publisher, I shall use the terms "early poems" and "1909 collection" synonymously to refer to these poems. Some poems in the group may well have been written several years before 1909, but the dating remains at best uncertain (see II, 28). Although little is known of the occasions for these poems, one thing is certain: nobody could have used them to predict the emergence of a major poet.

Despite the poor quality of the 1909 collection, some of the

central concerns of Trakl's later poetry are already evident in
his earliest surviving work. In a letter written to his older sister
Minna shortly after his arrival in Vienna in 1908, Trakl provides
a key to the basic thematic patterns of his poetry by describing
two sharply contrasting moods he has experienced:

I believe it must be terrible to live continually in full consciousness
of all the animal instincts which constantly whirl through life. I have
experienced, smelled, touched the most frightening possibilities within
myself, have heard the demons howling in my blood, the thousand
devils with their spurs which drive the flesh mad. What a horrible
nightmare!

Gone! Today this vision of reality has again sunk into nothing,
[these] things are far away from me, their voice still farther and I,
all living ear, again listen to the melodies inside me, and my wingèd
eye again dreams its images, which are more beautiful than all reality.

(I, 472)

Despite the highly conventional language of this letter—a
number of images and phrases directly echo a passage from
Hölderlin's novel *Hyperion*[2]—the contrast between malign and
idyllic moods was to become a controlling framework throughout
Trakl's poetry. In the early poem "Die drei Teiche in Hellbrunn"
("The Three Ponds in Hellbrunn"), the pond reflected in each
of the first two stanzas depicts one of these extreme moods in
symbolic terms:

Der Erste

Um die Blumen taumelt das Fliegengeschmeiss
Um die bleichen Blumen auf dumpfer Flut,
Geh fort! Geh fort! Es brennt die Luft!
In der Tiefe glüht der Verwesung Glut!
Die Weide weint, das Schweigen starrt,
Auf den Wassern braut ein schwüler Dunst.
Geh fort! Geh fort! Dies ist der Ort
Für schwarzer Kröten ekle Brunst.

Der Zweite

Bilder von Wolken, Blumen und Menschen—
Singe, singe, freudige Welt!
Lächelnde Unschuld spiegelt dich wider—
Himmlisch wird alles, was ihr gefällt:
Dunkles wandelt sie freundlich in Helle,

Fernes wird nah. O Freudiger du!
Sonne, Wolken, Blumen und Menschen
Atmen selig Gottesruh.

The First [Pond]

Around the flowers the fly-vermin reel,	x
Around the pale flowers on [the] murky waters,	a
Go away! Go away! The air is burning!	x
In the depths the glow of decay is glowing!	a
The willow weeps, the silence stares [stiffens],	x
On the waters a sultry vapor brews.	b
Go away! Go away! It is the place	x
For black toads' disgusting passion.	b

The Second [Pond]

Images of clouds, flowers, and people—
Sing, sing, joyful world!
Smiling innocence reflects you—
Everything it [innocence] likes becomes heavenly!
It [innocence] amicably transforms darkness into light,
Distant things become near! Oh joyful you!
Sun, clouds, flowers, and people
Breathe blissful peace in God.   (I, 238)

I should explain from the start that the banality of my
translation reflects the extreme banality of language in the
original. Yet like the immature work of most poets, "Die drei
Teiche in Hellbrunn" contains the essential thought structures
which were to govern Trakl's later and incomparably finer poetry.
In the above passages, the two contrasting aspects of reality—
corruption and death on the one hand, joyfulness and beauty on
the other—anticipate the opposing forces which were to control
the organization of his mature poems.[3] Although most of the
poems in the 1909 collection are not built as precisely on this
principle as "Die drei Teiche in Hellbrunn," the majority at
least give symbolic expression to one or the other of these two
states of mind.

Within these early poems, Trakl explores the negative side
of his poetic world much more thoroughly than he does the
positive; in fact, his most frequently recurring images are centered
around sickness, decay, and personal torment. Not only do we

encounter titles such as "Verfall" ("Decay" [I, 233]), and "Das Grauen" ("Horror" [I, 220]), but the poems themselves are full of lines such as "So spielt um kranke Blumen noch die Sonne" ("Thus the sun still plays about sick flowers" [I, 217]) and "Der Raum ist von Verwesung schwül" ("The room is close with corruption" [I, 233]); indeed, one can scarcely read a page without feeling satiated by the almost unremitting spectacle of horror and decay.

Yet occasionally Trakl suggests an atmosphere of unspoiled beauty similar to that in the second stanza of "Die drei Teiche in Hellbrunn," as, for instance, in the opening of the sonnet "Andacht" ("Devotion"), which evokes the Salzburg world of his childhood:

> Das Unverlorne meiner jungen Jahre
> Ist stille Andacht an ein Glockenläuten,
> An aller Kirchen dämmernde Altare
> Und ihrer blauen Kuppeln Himmelweiten.

> What remains unlost of my early years   a
> Is quiet devotion to the pealing of bells,   b
> To the twilit altars of all churches   a
> And their blue domes' heavenly expanses.   b
> (I, 221)

The third stanza of "Die drei Teiche in Hellbrunn" reflects still another dimension of Trakl's world, the transitional state between the two extremes:

Der Dritte

> Die Wasser schimmern grünlich-blau
> Und ruhig atmen die Zypressen,
> Es tönt der Abend glockentief—
> Da wächst die Tiefe unermessen.
> Der Mond steigt auf, es blaut die Nacht,
> Erblüht im Widerschein der Fluten—
> Ein rätselvolles Sphinxgesicht,
> Daran mein Herz sich will verbluten.

The Third [Pond]

> The waters shimmer greenish-blue
> And quietly the cypresses breathe,
> The evening sounds bell-deep—

> Then [there] the depths grow immeasurably.
> The moon rises, the night turns blue,
> Blossoms in the reflection of the waters—
> An enigmatic Sphinx face,
> On which my heart is about to bleed to death.
>
> (I, 238)

Whereas the first two stanzas had portrayed states of mind which remain fairly stable, the third creates images suggesting process and change. In subsequent years, Trakl was to revise the poem considerably, and his revision of the above lines indicates an attempt to find a more precise set of images for the transitional states. Thus, he replaced the third to sixth lines of the last stanza with the following:

> Und ihre Schwermut unermessen
> Fliesst über in das Abendblau.
> Tritonen tauchen aus der Flut,
> Verfall durchrieselt das Gemäuer
>
> And its immeasurable melancholy
> Overflows into the evening-blue.
> Tritons emerge from the waters,
> Decay flows through the masonry. . . .
>
> (I, 178)

In his early poetry, then, Trakl is concerned not merely with the extremes of decay and dissolution, but with the processes, often quite gentle and slow, by which these come about. Such verbs as "zerfliessen" ("dissolve," "melt away") and "gleiten" ("glide," "slip") are used throughout the 1909 collection to depict a world that is constantly undergoing change. In two poems, "Drei Traüme" ("Three Dreams" [I, 215]) and "Aus-klang" ("Dying Away" [I, 243]), he uses the image of falling leaves, thus foreshadowing his use of autumn as the most potent symbol of transition in his mature work.

The transition from a benign state to one of dissolution, which the third stanza of "Die drei Teiche in Hellbrunn" depicts, anticipates the characteristic organization of many of Trakl's later poems: for instance, "Elis" (I, 85-86), which, as I shall show in a subsequent chapter, enacts the transition from a state of perfection to one of total bleakness. But the reverse movement, from a negative to a positive state, is also present in many poems throughout his career, from the early "Gesang zur Nacht" ("Song to the Night" [I, 223-27]) to a later poem such as "Ein

Winterabend" ("A Winter Evening" [I, 102]), which depicts the arrival of a wanderer from dark snowy paths into a world of certainty and warmth.

Besides this play of opposites, the 1909 collection also displays the basic character types and dramatic situations which recur and are further developed in Trakl's later work. The two characters who dominate his poetic world from the start are, first, the speaker-protagonist, who assumes such semblances as criminal and sufferer as well as mere observer, and, second, the sister—in the early poems she is sometimes simply an anonymous woman—who appears variously as a victim of the protagonist's violence and as a partner in incest. The protagonist is often portrayed as a kind of double, as in the poem "Das Grauen," in which, after describing poisonous flowers growing out of his mouth, he suddenly recognizes himself in the mirror as Cain and concludes, "Da bin mit meinem Mörder ich allein" ("Then I am alone with my murderer" [I, 220]). In the poem "Naturtheater" ("Nature Theater" [I, 241]), moreover, he views the lost innocence of his childhood as though it were taking place before him on a stage. In the duality of character exemplified here, Trakl anticipates the far more complex late prose poem "Traum und Umnachtung" ("Dream and Madness" [I, 147-50]), in which the protagonist is fragmented among a number of roles, and, in the course of the poem, alternates constantly between a state of grace and damnation. For Trakl the polarities of character are at once polarities of the outer world.

The protagonist's role of sufferer—a common enough stance in fin de siècle poetry—is doubtless the role which he assumes most frequently in the early poems. In certain poems, the suffering is explicitly connected with feelings of guilt, perhaps most strikingly so in "Blutschuld" ("Incest"), whose opening stanza reads as follows:

> Es dräut die Nacht am Lager unsrer Küsse.
> Es flüstert wo: Wer nimmt von euch die Schuld?
> Noch bebend von verruchter Wollust Süsse
> Wir beten: Verzeih uns, Maria, in deiner Huld!

Night is threatening at the bed of our kisses.	a
Somewhere there whispers: Who [will] absolve your guilt?	b
Still quivering from the sweetness of heinous lust	a
We pray: forgive us, Mary, in your mercy!	b

(I, 249)

Trakl's incestuous relationship with his sister Grete, though it
is treated with varying degrees of directness from one poem
to the next, is one of the most persistent themes throughout
his work. Even at this early date, the writing of poetry was
for Trakl a way of coping with personal guilt, and he could
already have stated his poetics in terms similar to those he used
shortly before his death, when he handed Ludwig von Ficker
the awesome words quoted earlier: "Feeling in the moments of
death-like existence: All human beings are worthy of love.
Waking, you feel the world's bitterness; in this lies all your
unresolved guilt; your poem an imperfect atonement" (I, 463).

Just as the protagonist in Trakl's later poems moves from
one role to another, so the sister alternates among the extremes.
Innumerable later poems, for instance, end with a vision of
her transformed into a heavenly being. As in the case of
Goethe's Gretchen, whose name Trakl's sister shares, the protagonist's guilt is assuaged, as it were, by his assigning his victim
a divine role in the order of things. But this role is not yet
discernible in the 1909 collection. Instead, Trakl concentrates
on her role as victim, which sometimes takes the specific form
of an angry, wronged woman who sets off a reaction of guilt in
the protagonist as soon as she confronts him. Thus, at the end
of the sonnet "Andacht," the opening of which was quoted
earlier to exemplify Trakl's portrait of a still unspoiled world,
the protagonist is confronted with the frightening memory of
a woman:

> Da schimmert aus verworrenen Gestalten
> Ein Frauenbild, umflort von finstrer Trauer,
> Und giesst in mich den Kelch verruchter Schauer.
>
> Then from among confused figures there shimmers
> A woman's image, veiled with sinister mourning,
> And pours the chalice of heinous terrors into me.
>   (I, 221)

Throughout Trakl's work, the protagonist's sense of guilt is
associated not only with incest but also with murder and rape.
Trakl often, in fact, interchanges these crimes quite arbitrarily,
and in "Traum und Umnachtung," as I shall show, he depicts
all three within a single poem. Murder and rape are not explicit
in the 1909 collection, but they are central motifs in his two
extant dramatic attempts of this period. Of *Don Juans Tod*

(*Don Juan's Death* [I, 447-53]), only two short scenes and
some lines from a prologue survive, and although they tell us
next to nothing about the plot as a whole, they at least indicate
that Trakl's Don Juan, unlike the legend's traditional hero,
sadistically murders Donna Anna. The other dramatic piece,
Blaubart (*Bluebeard* [I, 435-45]), a one-act puppet play, deviates
significantly from its source, Maeterlinck's *Ariane et Barbe-Bleu*.
Whereas Maeterlinck's hero finds himself outwitted by his new
wife, Trakl's hero threatens his bride with extreme forms of
sadism, kills her, cries to God, and, in a final Dostoevskian
gesture, throws himself wildly before a crucifix.

Although Trakl's major themes (one might almost say ob-
sessions) are all present, in one way or another, in his early
work, his way of treating them differs radically from that characteristic of his mature period.[4] A conspicuous feature of the
style of his early verse, for example, is the predominant use
of the first person. Fully half of the lyrics that make up the
1909 collection contain the first-person pronoun within the two
opening lines, while many others are written in the second
person. In most of the mature works, on the other hand, he
maintains a posture of objectivity, recording images and events
usually in the third person and without the explicit intrusion of
a narrator. One need only compare the opening line of one
early poem, "Mich däucht, ich träumte von Blätterfall" ("I
thought I dreamt of the falling of leaves" [I, 215]), in which
the poet imposes two first-person pronouns before the image,
with the far more directly presented "Alte Plätze sonnig
schweigen" ("Old squares are sunnily silent" [I, 23]), which
opens "Die schöne Stadt" ("The Beautiful City"), a poem
written within a year of the earlier one.

Closely connected with this subjectivity in the early poems
is his use of conventional embellishments. Here, to a far greater
degree than in his later work, Trakl utilizes the various lyrical
conventions established in German poetry since the Romantic
period. We find, for instance, an extensive use of the refrain,
as in "Blutschuld," where the mood of horror is all but broken
by means of the songlike repetitions of "Forgive us, Mary, in
your mercy" (I, 249). In the last of the "Gesang zur Nacht"
("Song to the Night") poems, the refrain, "Du bist in tiefer
Mitternacht" ("You are in deep midnight" [I, 227]), takes up
fully half of the twelve lines.

Nowhere in the later poetry, moreover, do we find the variety of traditional metrical forms that make up the 1909 collection. The poems of the three succeeding years consist largely of sonnets and groups of rhymed quatrains, while during 1913-14, the years of his poetic maturity, he wrote mainly free verse and prose poems. But in the 1909 collection, besides the large numbers of sonnets and series of quatrains, we find several poems in rhymed tercets, two in blank verse, and several in rhymed six- and eight-foot stanzas. Of the dramas, *Don Juans Tod*—at least what remains of it—is mainly in blank verse, while *Blaubart* is in *Knittelversen*, the rough-hewn, doggerellike form which Goethe had employed in many parts of *Faust*.

Trakl's diction, too, shows major differences between the early and later styles. A word count made some years ago of most of Trakl's poems after 1909 can help us chart these differences.[5] Thus, of the ten most frequently recurring nouns and adjectives in the mature poetry, only two, "Nacht" ("night") and "dunkel" ("dark"), are used with any real frequency in the early poems. On the other hand, the word "schwarz" ("black"), used more than a hundred times—more frequently than any noun or any other adjective—in the later poems, cannot be found at all in the 1909 collection. This difference in poetic language does not, however, imply any corresponding lack of thematic continuity in Trakl's work. Rather, in his increasing search for more oblique ways of expression, words like "schwarz" come to connote many of the negative qualities which words like "krank" ("sick"), "Grauen" ("horror"), and "verrucht" ("heinous") suggested in his early work.

Another significant stylistic difference between the two periods is Trakl's use of general, often declamatory, statements instead of concrete images in the early poems. One might compare, for instance, the third line of "Blutschuld," "Noch bebend von verruchter Wollust Süsse" ("Still quivering from the sweetness of heinous lust" [I, 249]), with some far more concrete lines from "Passion," a late poem also concerned with incest:

> Unter finsteren Tannen
> Mischten zwei Wölfe ihr Blut
> In steinerner Umarmung.

> Under dark firs
> Two wolves mixed their blood
> In a stony embrace.   (I, 125)

In the earlier line, Trakl still depends on conventional poetic diction, heavy-handedly trying to describe a complex emotional situation from the outside. In "Passion," instead of such empty abstractions as "sweetness" and "heinous lust," Trakl lets the images define the situation for the reader. The dark trees at once introduce a sense of foreboding, while the words "Wölfe" ("wolves") and "Blut" ("blood")—joined as they are by "mischten" ("mixed"), with its suggestion of brute mechanical process— serve, in their oblique way, both to enact a situation and to define the poet's attitude toward it. But it is only in the third line, with its unexpected combination of "steinern" ("stony") and "Umarmung" ("embrace"), that Trakl suggests the full horror of the incestuous relationship. Such complexity (which is the very life of Trakl's mature art) is entirely missing in his early work. Instead, the young poet seemed to content himself with some of the most worn-out expressions for strong emotion in German poetry—such a phrase as "Zerwühlt, verzerrt bist du von jedem Schmerz" ("You are rooted up and torn out of shape by every pain" [I, 218]) offering an easy substitute for a concretely embodied situation. In one poem, perhaps at a loss for something more specific, he even speaks of "mystische Unendlichkeiten" ("mystic infinities" [I, 254]).

This is not to say that abstractions are totally lacking in his later work; but when they occur they are always fused with concrete imagery. Compare, for instance, the opening line of "Klage" ("Lament"), one of his two last poems, with the line from "Blutschuld" which I have already quoted twice, "Still quivering from the sweetness of heinous lust":

> Des Menschen goldnes Bildnis
> Verschlänge die eisige Woge
> Der Ewigkeit.

> The icy wave of eternity
> Would [might] swallow
> Man's golden image,
>
> (I, 166)

In the early poem, Trakl depends totally on the abstraction "heinous lust" to raise the emotional pitch. In the later poem, by contrast, the abstraction "eternity" is absorbed, as it were, within the image of the ravenous icy wave. The early poems, to be sure, also contain innumerable concrete images, but all

too often, as in the lines "Dumpfe Fieberglut / Lässt giftige
Blumen blühn aus meinem Munde" ("A stifling fever-glow causes
poisonous flowers to bloom from my mouth" [I, 220]), the effect
of Trakl's concrete images is as embarrassing as is that of his
abstractions.

Trakl's advance in technique can also be illustrated if one
compares the early version of "Die drei Teiche in Hellbrunn"
with one of its subsequent revisions. Here are the opening lines
of the first version:

> Um die Blumen taumelt das Fliegengeschmeiss
> Um die bleichen Blumen auf dumpfer Flut,
> Geh fort! Geh fort! Es brennt die Luft!
> In der Tiefe glüht der Verwesung Glut!
>
> Around the flowers the fly-vermin reel,
> Around the pale flowers on [the] murky waters,
> Go away! Go away! The air is burning!
> In the depths the glow of decay is glowing!

When changed, they create a more controlled and subdued, and
ultimately more terrifying effect:

> Umgaukelt von gräulichem Fliegengeschmeiss
> Gleiten Masken auf brauner Flut,
> Kleine Hände verstorben und weiss
> Und wärmen sich an der Verwesung Glut.
>
> Hovered over by gruesome fly-vermin
> Masks glide on brown waters,
> Little hands dead and white
> And warm themselves on the glow of the decay.
>   (II, 357)

Whereas the early version resorted to exclamations for an effect
of horror, the later one achieves this effect with far greater
precision by means of concrete images presented in a calm,
descriptive manner. Moreover, by substituting "hands" and
"masks" for "flowers," Trakl not only portrays the process of
decay more forcefully than in his original image, but he also
utilizes an extreme form of figurative language that was not to
become prevalent in his work until the last two years.[6]

The second stanza is entirely rewritten in the second version,
with such generalities and clichés as

> Singe, singe, freudige Welt!
> Lächelnde Unschuld spiegelt dich wider—
> Himmlisch wird alles, was ihr gefällt:
>
> Sing, sing, joyful world!
> Smiling innocence reflects you—
> Everything it [innocence] likes becomes heavenly!

making way for these specific images:

> Stimmen von Frauen, die längst verstarben
> Weben zärtlich und dunkelfarben
> Über dem weissen nymphischen Spiegel.
>
> Voices of women who died long ago
> Hover delicately and dark-colored
> Over the white nymphlike mirror.
>
>   (I, 178)

In order to find concrete images for a "positive" vision to counteract the "negative" world of the first stanza, Trakl here attempts to re-create the loveliness of Hellbrunn's past. Hellbrunn (where one can still see the three reflecting pools on which Trakl based his poem) is a Renaissance-style castle built by the reigning prince-archbishop of Salzburg outside the city in the early seventeenth century. Not only in this later version, but in many other poems written before 1911, Trakl constantly drew visual images from his native city—its statuary, fountains, formal gardens, churches, palaces—to evoke its past glories.

Yet the very pastness of this world undercuts its adequacy as a "positive" symbol. The "delicate" voices in the lines quoted above are, after all, the voices of women who died long ago. However beautiful the mythological statues that recur in poem after poem may still seem, Trakl usually reminds us that they are falling into ruin. The "positive" concrete images which Trakl draws from the world around him are, in short, as notable for their transitoriness as for their beauty. The ambiguity inherent in such images, moreover, is typical of the sort of ambiguity which he was to exploit throughout his subsequent work.

II *The Rhymed Poems of 1909-12: "Die schöne Stadt," "Menschliches Elend," and "Menschheit"*

The concreteness, impersonality, and precision evident in the revised passages of "Die drei Teiche in Hellbrunn" I have quoted are the dominant characteristics in all of Trakl's poetry from late 1909 until the end of 1912, when, as I shall show in detail in the next chapter, his work took a radical turn in a new direction. These characteristics are so persistent throughout this period that, whenever external evidence is missing (as indeed it is in most instances), exact dates for the poems written in these three years can rarely be assigned. If anything, one can say that Trakl moves toward ever greater concreteness and toward a context of more complex and closely crowded meanings. At one point during this period, he wrote to Buschbeck to justify his revision of a poem: "It is better than the original to the degree that it is now impersonal, and full, to the bursting point, of movement and visions" (I, 485). The poem he was discussing, "Klagelied" ("Lamentation" [I, 280]), is, I might add, one of his weakest compositions. Yet his evident intent to subordinate personal commentary and reflection to the recording of things directly—or the "infernal chaos of rhythms and images" of which he speaks in another letter (I, 479)—at once points up the difference between the early poems and those of the subsequent period. In the letter discussing "Klagelied" he goes on to write, "You may well believe me that I do not find it easy and never will find it easy to subordinate myself unconditionally to the object to be represented, and I shall continually have to correct myself to give the truth its due" (I, 486). The objective presentation of what he sees and feels becomes, in effect, a way of getting to the truth of things. The worn-out conventions and clichéd language of the earlier poems were obviously unable to define his peculiar ways of thinking and feeling with any verbal precision; the concrete images out of which his subsequent poems are built become a way not only of recording the reality which he experiences, but because of his refusal to make these images subservient to any general statements, they also become a means of exploring the complexities of his inner world.

"Die schöne Stadt" ("The Beautiful City"), written between mid-1909 and mid-1910, is a fair representation of his new manner at a relatively early stage:

> Alte Plätze sonnig schweigen.
> Tief in Blau und Gold versponnen
> Traumhaft hasten sanfte Nonnen
> Unter schwüler Buchen Schweigen.

Aus den braun erhellten Kirchen
Schaun des Todes reine Bilder,
Grosser Fürsten schöne Schilder.
Kronen schimmern in den Kirchen.

Rösser tauchen aus dem Brunnen.
Blütenkrallen drohn aus Bäumen.
Knaben spielen wirr von Träumen
Abends leise dort am Brunnen.

Mädchen stehen an den Toren,
Schauen scheu ins farbige Leben.
Ihre feuchten Lippen beben
Und sie warten an den Toren.

Zitternd flattern Glockenklänge,
Marschtakt hallt und Wacherufen.
Fremde lauschen auf den Stufen.
Hoch im Blau sind Orgelklänge.

Helle Instrumente singen.
Durch der Gärten Blätterrahmen
Schwirrt das Lachen schöner Damen.
Leise junge Mütter singen.

Heimlich haucht an blumigen Fenstern
Duft von Weihrauch, Teer und Flieder.
Silbern flimmern müde Lider
Durch die Blumen an den Fenstern.

1	Old squares are sunnily silent.	a
2	Deeply entangled in blue and gold	b
3	Gentle nuns hurry dreamily	b
4	Under the silence of sultry beech trees.	a

5   Out of the brownly illuminated churches
6   Death's pure images gaze,
7   Great princes' beautiful coats of arms.
8   Crowns glimmer in the churches.

9   Horses emerge out of the fountain.
10 Blossom claws threaten from trees.
11 Boys, confused by dreams, are playing
12 In the evening softly there at the fountain.

13   Girls stand at the gateways,
14   Gaze timidly into the colorful life.
15   Their moist lips quiver
16   And they wait at the gateways.

17   Bell-sounds flutter trembling,
18   March rhythm sounds and calling of the guard.
19   Strangers listen on the steps.
20   High in the blue are organ sounds.

21   Bright instruments sing.
22   Through the gardens' borders [frames] of foliage
23   The laughing of beautiful ladies whirs by
24   Quietly [quiet] young mothers sing.

25   Stealthily at flowery windows there breathes
26   Smell of incense, tar, and lilacs.
27   Silver-like, tired eyelids flicker
28   Through the flowers at the windows.

                                                    (I, 23-24)

The poem consists of series of ostensibly objective images, whose only discernible connection is that they center around the sights and sounds, persons and places of a single city, the Salzburg of Trakl's youth. To borrow Trakl's own phrasing from the letter quoted above, the poet fully subordinates himself here to the object he is representing. Assuming the role of impersonal observer, he records, apparently in no set order, the objects he sees and hears about him. The poem has no real beginning nor end. Stanzas could be interchanged or even omitted without changing the poem radically. At this point in his career, Trakl evidently conceived of the stanza—rather than the line or the total poem—as his central unit of meaning. Thus, in a letter concerning another poem ("Der Gewitterabend"—"The Evening Thunderstorm" [I, 27]), he speaks of his "plastic [*bildhafte*] manner, which in the four lines of the stanza fuses together four individual components of an image [*Bildteile*] into a single impression" (I, 478).

In "Die schöne Stadt," the stanza, through the repetition of the last word of the opening line in the fourth line, achieves even greater unity than in the poem Trakl was describing in the letter. Thus, in the final stanza, he moves from "flowery windows" to various kinds of smells, and then to the "flickering" of "tired eyelids"; but in the fourth line he lets the stanza come to rest, as it were, with the repetition of the image of the "flowers at the windows." One might describe the effect of this stanza as follows: first a gradual widening of the reader's range of vision, as the poet introduces such disparate phenomena as incense, tar, and lilacs; and then, through the repetition at the end, an attempt to fuse these images into "a single impression," as Trakl puts it in his letter.

The objectivity with which the observing poet records his images is of course only a relative one. The line "Girls stand at the gate-ways" (I, 13) is objective enough, for it gives only the essentials of what he observes. The following line not only interprets the expressions on the girls' faces, but, in qualifying the life into which they gaze as "colorful," he is, in effect, reflecting upon the nature of things. No less subjective is his use of the word "stealthily" in the final stanza to describe the smell blowing along the windows. Yet despite these subjective touches, he never fully destroys the illusion that the images exist independently of the poet.

The word "image" is, to be sure, only an approximate term for the components of this poem, though Trakl himself used the term—"Bild" in German—to describe his style during this period. "Die schöne Stadt" is composed of images to the extent that the poet represents objects discernible to the senses. But one might just as well use the word "event" to describe the units out of which the poem is built, for each unit contains a verb and sometimes, as in the last three lines of the first stanza, an extended predicate. Indeed, the reader is often more clearly aware of the action of the verbs than of the nouns they set in motion. Nuns are hurrying, eyelids flicker, laughter whirs by, and the young girls, though standing still, are waiting and gazing *into* the "colorful life." One constantly has the impression of something—in fact, many things—about to happen, yet never reaching fulfillment, for the poet shifts his vision to new objects before he can complete the actions implied in the preceding ones. The world he portrays is one of constant movement, even though he achieves a sense of temporary stasis in every stanza through the repeated word in the last line.

On first reading, one might think of "Die schöne Stadt" as a depiction of the "positive" side of Trakl's world. The word "beautiful" in the title, the crowns shimmering in the churches,

the haunting sounds of march rhythms, laughter, and young
mothers singing—all help create a fully realized impression of
loveliness. But the sense of movement that dominates the poem
throughout serves also to qualify the loveliness which Trakl is
at such pains to depict. Or, to put it another way, things are
lovely in the world of this poem only to the extent that they
are transitory; yet their very transitoriness is a reminder of the
death and decay which threaten all lovely things. The princely
coats of arms and the ancient crowns in the second stanza owe
much of their sensuous appeal to our knowledge that they are
all that remain of a lost world; the very phrase with which Trakl
introduces them, "Death's pure images," brings their positive
and negative aspects together at once.

Trakl attempted a similar fusion of the positive and negative
in the line "Blossom claws threaten from trees," in the succeeding
stanza, but this line still seems to me—after years of reading
the poem—a serious breach of tact in an otherwise successful
poem. Although Trakl was later to gain great mastery in effecting
this kind of fusion, the intrusion here of "blossom claws threaten-
ing" is too sudden, too direct: the delicate balance between the
presence of beauty and its transitoriness breaks down. Indeed,
through its delicacy of tone the poem becomes essentially an
elegy for a transient world of loveliness. As such, it belongs to
a tradition established in German by poets of a slightly older
generation—for instance, by Hofmannsthal in his "Terzinen:
Über Vergänglichkeit" ("Tercets: On Transitoriness") and Stefan
George in his early poem "Hochsommer" ("Midsummer"), whose
images and rhythms are closely akin to Trakl's:

> Ton verklang auf den altanen·
> Aus den gärten klänge tönen·
> Unter prangenden platanen
> Wiegen sich die stolzen Schönen·

Sound died out on the balconies·	a
Sounds ring from gardens·	b
Under magnificent plane trees	a
The proud beautiful women are swaying.[7]	b

Like Hofmannsthal and George before him, Trakl has fashioned
a poetry of gardens, lovely ladies, and dying sounds to commemorate a swiftly passing reality. The elegiac tone which
controls Trakl's "objective" stance in "Die schöne Stadt" antici-

pates the characteristic tone which he assumes throughout most of his subsequent poems. To elegize is to recognize the precariousness of objects and thus to capture them, if possible, in their immediacy: things become more concrete and precise for us to the degree that we are made to see how very temporary they are. In "Elis," a poem written at least three years after "Die schöne Stadt," the elegiac tone is still dominant:

> Ein blaues Wild
> Blutet leise im Dornengestrüpp.
>
> Ein brauner Baum steht abgeschieden da;
> Seine blauen Früchte fielen von ihm.
>
> A blue animal [deer]
> Bleeds softly in the bramble bushes.
>
> A brown tree stands there dead [secluded];
> Its blue fruits fell down from it.
>
> (I, 86)

What separates a poem like "Elis" from "Die schöne Stadt" is not the tone (which, however, is much more subtly manipulated in the later poem) but the fact that the earlier poem describes a real and recognizable world. The children, the soldiers, and the churches of "Die schöne Stadt" seem far less removed from everyday reality than the bramble bushes, the bleeding animals, and the blue imagery of the later poem.

Yet even the images of "Die schöne Stadt" have a touch of unreality about them; the boys are "confused by dreams," the bell sounds "tremble" and "flutter," the nuns hurry along in a "dreamlike" way. Indeed, everything takes place in a kind of dreamlike state, but at the same time one never forgets the presence of the daylight, the power of which is stressed in the opening line by the word "sonnig" ("sunny"), a word conspicuous here because it is syntactically displaced and functions as an adverb. Even though the stanzas seem to be in no particularly relevant order, the poem achieves a unity through a common atmosphere which surrounds and shapes the various scenes. It is an atmosphere, moreover, which seems to create its own world, one composed not only of the dreamlike movements and the daylight but also of a sense of quiet, as is evident from the start through the repeated rhyme word "Schweigen" ("silence"

—used here as both a verb and a noun, respectively) in the opening stanza. The word "leise" ("quiet," "soft") occurs twice, and the various verbs, for all their effect of motion, suggest quiet, gentle movements. Even the music—for instance the organ sounds heard "high in the blue" or the singing of "quiet young mothers"— seems relatively subdued. One also notes a preponderance of unvoiced consonants, as in the line "Kronen schimmern in den Kirchen." The hushed quality is so persistent that one senses a certain mysteriousness about the poem as a whole; one feels throughout, in fact, that one mode of reality is about to give way to another. This sense of imminent change is, indeed, common to all of Trakl's poems, for all, in one way or another, are concerned with processes of transition, with the movement of one state of being toward its opposite.

Still, though the reader is always aware of the precariousness of things in "Die schöne Stadt," the predominant tone of the poem is relatively positive. Quite in contrast, a poem such as "Menschliches Elend" ("Human Misery"), as the title indicates from the start, contains images of a distinctly negative nature:

Die Uhr, die vor der Sonne fünfe schlägt—
Einsame Menschen packt ein dunkles Grausen,
Im Abendgarten kahle Bäume sausen.
Des Toten Antlitz sich am Fenster regt.

Vielleicht, dass diese Stunde stille steht.
Vor trüben Augen blaue Bilder gaukeln
Im Takt der Schiffe, die am Flusse schaukeln.
Am Kai ein Schwesternzug vorüberweht.

Im Hasel spielen Mädchen blass und blind,
Wie Liebende, die sich im Schlaf umschlingen.
Vielleicht, daß um ein Aas dort Fliegen singen,
Vielleicht auch weint im Mutterschoss ein Kind.

Aus Händen sinken Astern blau und rot,
Des Jünglings Mund entgleitet fremd und weise;
Und Lider flattern angstverwirrt und leise;
Durch Fieberschwärze weht ein Duft von Brot.

Es scheint, man hört auch grässliches Geschrei;
Gebeine durch verfallne Mauern schimmern.
Ein böses Herz lacht laut in schönen Zimmern;
An einem Träumer läuft ein Hund vorbei.

Ein leerer Sarg im Dunkel sich verliert.
Dem Mörder will ein Raum sich bleich erhellen,
Indes Laternen nachts im Sturm zerschellen.
Des Edlen weisse Schläfe Lorbeer ziert.

1 The clock that strikes five before sunrise—   a
2 A dark terror grips lonely people,   b
3 In the evening-garden, bare trees whistle.   b
4 The dead man's face stirs at the window.   a

5 It may be that this hour is standing still.
6 Before dull eyes blue images flutter
7 To the rhythm of the ships which rock in the river.
8 At the wharf a troop of nuns blows by.

9 In the hazel bush girls play pale and blind,
10 Like lovers who embrace in sleep.
11 Perhaps flies are singing there around a carcass,
12 Perhaps also a child is weeping in its mother's lap.

13 Asters fall blue and red from hands,
14 The youth's mouth slips away strange and wise;
15 And eyelids flutter fear-confused and softly;
16 A scent of bread blows through fever-blackness.

17 It seems that one hears also horrible screaming;
18 Bones [skeletons] glimmer through ruined walls.
19 An evil heart laughs loudly in beautiful rooms;
20 A dog runs past a dreamer.

21 An empty coffin disappears in the dark.
22 A room [area] is about to light up for the murderer,
23 While lanterns are shattered in the storm at night.
24 Laurel decorates the nobleman's white temple.

(I, 62)

This version of "Menschliches Elend" could have been written anywhere from late 1910 to early 1912, though, as with many other Trakl poems, it is based on an earlier poem and was revised again much later. At two points in this poem, Trakl echoes lines from "Die schöne Stadt," first the images of nuns "blowing" by along the wharf (1. 8 of this poem and 1. 3 of the earlier one) and, next, the image of eyelids fluttering" (11. 15 and 27, respectively). The difference in the way these images are used in each poem defines the difference in emphasis between the two. Although both poems are concerned with processes of transition, the words "dreamlike" and "gentle," with which the nuns are depicted in the first poem, as well as the flowers at the windows through which the "tired eyelids" gaze, stress the positive aspect of these processes. By contrast, the world of "Menschliches Elend" seems uncompromisingly bleak: the eyelids are "confused by fear"; and the nuns "blow by," as though at the mercy of an infernal, Dantesque wind.[8]

If the poem has any unity at all, this unity resides in the sense of dread which holds the images together in much the same way that the fading beauties of Salzburg serve as a kind of common denominator to describe "Die schöne Stadt." But this is a questionable unity at best. Except for the rhyme words, most of the lines could be shifted to other parts of the poem, or, for that matter, to other poems. One does not have to read very far in Trakl to note that the same words and images recur persistently from poem to poem: indeed, after years of reading Trakl I must confess that I still have trouble remembering what line belongs to what poem. The word "unity," whatever its relevance as a critical term for earlier modes of poetry, is useful only to a limited degree in discussing an individual Trakl poem. Through the poet's dependence on concrete images and through the ambiguities which he cultivates by means of these images, many of his poems have a kind of "open-endedness" which an earlier esthetic would never have tolerated.

Thus, even Trakl's rhymed quatrains provide only a semblance of unity for the lines of any particular stanza. Despite his avowal, in the letter previously quoted, that the individual quatrain represents a fusion of several images, or parts of an image, the individual line rather than the quatrain is the central unit of meaning in a poem such as "Menschliches Elend." If I may borrow a term used by Walter Höllerer to describe Trakl's style in another poem ("Trübsinn" ["Melancholy"—I, 53]) of this period, the individual poem is like a merry-go-round in which one image succeeds the other without any apparent connection between the two.[9]

One could say, of course, that the title "Menschliches Elend" connects the images, since they are all, in one way or another, examples of "human misery." But the title, whether it designates "human misery," "melancholy," or, to cite some other titles, "soul of life" or "evening muse," has at best only a loose meta-phorical connection with what follows. Even the opening line of "Menschliches Elend," with its designation of a particular time of day, has no real relationship with the succeeding lines: one can hardly expect the pale blind girls in the third stanza to be playing in hazel bushes at five in the morning!

Yet the very looseness of form implicit in Trakl's "merry-go-round" manner is an index to the meanings he attempts to convey. The various images flash by as though the poet were implying that he could not bring them under any effective control. In his role of "objective" observer, he is every bit as removed from his creation as is the deity standing behind the world which is depicted here. In fact, through the word "viel-leicht" ("perhaps") with which three lines (11. 5, 11, and 12) are introduced, and the phrase "es scheint" ("it seems"), which opens another (l. 17), the poet indicates his powerlessness adequately to visualize the world before him.

To the extent that "Menschliches Elend" is a poem about processes of transition, it is also a poem about the relentless flow of time. It is notable that, except for a single run-on line (11. 6-7), every image or event fills the same amount of space and follows much the same metrical pattern: the regularity, indeed the monotony, inherent in this style, suggests the mechan-ical, merciless way with which time moves in the world created in this poem. Even the one line speculating that "this hour is standing still" (l. 5) seems grossly ironic in a context where it is obvious that nothing stands still, that things, in fact, rush on to their destruction without anything—be it God or the poet— to hold them back.

Through the distance he maintains from his images, the poet is able to avoid committing himself to too narrow a set of meanings. Thus, despite the prevailing negative tone, many images seem distinctly ambiguous in their effect. The beautiful and the ugly, the pleasant and the unpleasant, are often fused together in a single image. The evil heart, for instance, laughs in beautiful rooms (l. 19); the lovers in one another's arms (l. 10) seem caught in their guilt and their glory at once. The image that describes a dog running past the dreamer is neither positive nor negative but is simply an incongruous picture. The final line, with its laurel wreath decorating a noble person's forehead, can be taken as either positive or absurd. For that matter, any of these images may have had private meanings for Trakl that we can never quite recapture. To the degree that an image seems to become autonomous of its creator, it also achieves a certain complexity: without rhetorical control from the outside, its meanings can go in several directions at once.

But the autonomy of the images also has the effect of distancing the reader from them to an extent commensurate with their distance from the poet. The reader, in fact, remains curiously unmoved by the individual situations recorded in the poem. He may experience an occasional sense of horror, as in the image of the empty coffin (1. 21); or he may be impressed by the sheer power of a line, as for instance, "Einsame Menschen packt ein dunkles Grausen" ("A dark terror grips lonely people");[10] or he may feel disgust at the entire spectacle. But for a poem entitled "Human Misery," the various personages who are described excite a surprisingly small amount of sympathy. Given the nature of its subject matter, the poem seems notable for its refusal to be sentimental in any way.

That Trakl felt a special attachment to "Menschliches Elend" is evident from the fact that he radically revised it only a week before his suicide and at least a month after he had written his last two poems, "Klage" and "Grodek." His attachment seems all the more surprising since he had abandoned the style of "Menschliches Elend" some two years before. The revised poem, which consists of four stanzas rather than the six in the first two versions, is implicitly a criticism of the earlier versions from the standpoint of his later manner. The title, for one thing, is now changed to "Menschliche Trauer" ("Human Grief"). The shift from misery to grief indicates the more formal, lofty language of his final period. The first two stanzas are unchanged, except for the substitution of two words to render the tone more negative: the word "kahl" ("bare"—1. 3) is replaced by "morsch" ("rotting"), while "blau" ("blue"—1. 6), a very positive word in Trakl's vocabulary, gives way to the more ambiguous "nächtige" ("nocturnal"). The two middle stanzas are eliminated entirely, as a result of which the new poem, despite its random images, comes to seem relatively compact. The last two stanzas, moreover, are thoroughly rewritten:

> Es scheint, man hört der Fledermäuse Schrei,
> Im Garten einen Sarg zusammenzimmern.

Gebeine durch verfallne Mauern schimmern
Und schwärzlich schwankt ein Irrer dort vorbei.

Ein blauer Strahl im Herbstgewölk erfriert.
Die Liebenden im Schlafe sich umschlingen,
Gelehnet an der Engel Sternenschwingen,
Des Edlen bleiche Schläfe Lorbeer ziert.

It seems one hears the bats' screaming,	a
[And] in the garden a coffin being put together.	b
Bones [skeletons] glimmer through ruined walls	b
And blackly a madman sways past [over] there.	a

A blue ray freezes in the autumnal clouds.
The lovers embrace in their sleep,
Leaning on the angels' star-pinions,
Laurel decorates the nobleman's pale temple.

(I, 370)

Trakl's changes in these stanzas reflect his growth during the long period that intervened between the second and the final version. The change from "grässliches" ("horrible") to "Fledermäuse" ("bats") to describe the screaming is a criticism of the vagueness implicit in the word "grässlich," which is as overused in German as its equivalent in English. The lines about the "evil heart laughing in beautiful rooms" (1. 19) and the murderer in the room being lit up (1. 22) are eliminated because they display a melodramatic, distinctly "literary" quality which the later Trakl would not have tolerated. The swaying madman of the new version carries a more clearly absurd meaning than the dreamer (1. 20) of the earlier ones. The lovers and the laurel-wreathed nobleman, whose status seemed rather ambiguous in the earlier version, are elevated in the new final stanza through their association with "angels' star-pinions." The latter phrase, a stylization characteristic of the later Trakl, gives the poem a more positive note than anything in the earlier version. The mixture of styles, moreover, is not in the least disturbing, for the connections between images are loose enough to make room for a vast variety of additions and substitutions.

In his "merry-go-round" poems Trakl seems closer than at any other period of his career to the poet Georg Heym (1887-1912), his exact contemporary, with whom he has customarily been linked in literary histories and whose stature, until the relatively

recent acceptance of Trakl as a major poet, seemed equal to
Trakl's. The concreteness and precision of the following stanza
from Heym's "Die Heimat der Toten" ("The Home of the
Dead") approaches Trakl's manner:

> Ein altes totes Weib mit starkem Bauch,
> Das einen kleinen Kinderleichnam trägt.
> Er zieht die Brust wie einen Gummischlauch,
> Die ohne Milch und welk herunterschlägt.

> An old dead woman with a big belly,   a
> Who carries a small child's corpse.   b
> It pulls her breast like a rubber hose   a
> Which dangles, withered and without milk.[11]   b

Heym's unit of meaning is not the individual line—as is Trakl's
in most poems of this period—but the stanza. And the apparent
randomness of movement which characterizes Trakl's poems from
one line to the next is analogous to a randomness of movement
from one stanza to the next in Heym. Although it is easy enough
to tell both poets apart, the parallels between the two are
obviously striking: the relative autonomy of their images; the
common themes of urban misery, emptiness, decay, of cataclysms
about to take place; the dreamlike, even demonic quality that
often makes the world they are describing so concretely seem
unreal. Yet I know of no evidence to suggest that Heym exerted
any influence on Trakl's manner, for Trakl had already developed
this manner by the time Heym's work first became known. But
both poets, one might add, were working within a common
literary tradition. Both, for instance, felt the impact of Baudelaire's city poems and of Émile Verhaeren's compassionate poems
about the poor; both, moreover, were deeply influenced by
Rimbaud's famous poem about Ophelia's rotting corpse floating
downstream.[12] A fascination with decaying things, the fear of
coming war, the sense that an old order was breaking up—these
themes were very much in the air at the time, as most any
selection of serious German writing during those years will
readily show.

In the autumn of 1912 Trakl began experimenting in various
new directions and was gradually discarding the "merry-go-
round" manner of the preceding years. The central direction
in which he was to go, as I shall indicate in the following
chapter, was a form of free verse that strained the German

language more radically than that of any major poet before him. During the very period that he developed his free-verse style, he wrote several rhymed poems that show a tightness of organization which is completely different from the calculated randomness that characterizes the form of his poems in the preceding three years. Among them the exquisite five-line poem "Rondel" (I, 21), entitled simply after its metrical form, and the eight-line "Trompeten" ("Trumpets" [I, 47]), with its systematic word repetitions, achieve an artful, finely wrought effect which, except for the familiar vocabulary, one would not easily identify as Trakl's. Although his letters of the period give no hint of what he was trying to do, one suspects that he was uncertain at this point whether to develop within traditional forms or to move toward the autonomous image possible within free verse. The greatest of these rhymed poems seems to me "Menschheit" ("Mankind"), which creates a miniature drama within its ten lines:

> Menschheit vor Feuerschlünden aufgestellt,
> Ein Trommelwirbel, dunkler Krieger Stirnen,
> Schritte durch Blutnebel; schwarzes Eisen schellt,
> Verzweiflung, Nacht in traurigen Gehirnen:
> Hier Evas Schatten, Jagd und rotes Geld.
> Gewölk, das Licht durchbricht, das Abendmahl,
> Es wohnt in Brot und Wein ein sanftes Schweigen
> Und jene sind versammelt zwölf an Zahl.
> Nachts schrein im Schlaf sie unter Ölbaumzweigen;
> Sankt Thomas taucht die Hand ins Wundenmal.

1	Mankind ranged before cannons [fiery gorges],	a
2	A drum-roll, dark warriors' foreheads,	b
3	Strides through blood-fog; black iron is ringing;	a
4	Despair, night in sad brains:	b
5	Here Eve's shadow, hunting, and red money.	a
6	Clouds which light breaks through, the Last Supper.	c
7	There dwells in bread and wine a gentle silence.	d
8	And these are gathered twelve in number.	c
9	At night they scream in their sleep under olive branches;	d
10	Saint Thomas dips his hand into the stigmata.	c

(I, 43)

The spareness and economy of these lines, with their stark images and closely organized rhymes, are central to the effect they produce; in sharp contrast to most of Trakl's earlier poetry, not a line could be omitted or displaced without ruining this effect. In its finely worked out organization and its combination of sharp visual details with constant dramatic intensification, this is a Parnassian poem which shares a tradition with many of Rilke's *Neue Gedichte* (*New Poems*) and Yeats's "Leda and the Swan." Thematically, moreover, it is one of the great pre-World War I war poems which, like Georg Heym's most famous poem, "Der Krieg" ("War"), succeeds in evoking the horrors of modern war more powerfully than any of the German poems that were to come out of the war itself.

The first three lines list the particulars of war in rapid, unconnected phrases which overpower the reader by their concreteness and immediacy. Even the abstract opening word gains a terrifying concreteness through the brute effect of the words "aufgestellt" ("ranged," "set up") and "Feuerschlünde" (an epithet for "cannon" which means literally "fiery gorges"); one is able, in fact, to visualize millions of people herded before massive guns.

The relatively abstract words of the fourth line are both a summation of the preceding lines and a preparation for the new elements about to be introduced.[13] Every new element in the poem, moreover, serves as a comment on the events of the opening lines, for with each shift of direction we reach a new level of awareness. The images of the fifth line are different in kind from those of the opening lines. All are concrete embodiments of evil, but they are concrete in a peculiarly emblematic, allegorical way. Eve's shadow is an obvious enough emblem; "red money" suggests Judas; and "hunting" is a private image which Trakl frequently uses to connote terror and brutality. The emblematic quality of the line not only serves to comment on the evil nature of the events in the opening lines; it is also a sign that these events must be seen through a higher spiritual perspective. The sixth line presents another religious emblem, the Last Supper, which is as "positive" in nature as Eve's shadow or Judas' money are "negative." This sudden shift seems plausible, partly through our automatic association of Judas with the Last Supper, but also, I suspect, through Trakl's staging a vision in the clouds with a Baroque theatricality which we are willing to accept on account of the very shamelessness of its artifice.

With this shift toward the positive, we are ready for the specific image of the sacrament in the seventh line. This image is

the poem's still center, "still," in fact, in the most literal sense
of the word through the static quality of "wohnt" ("dwells") and
"sanftes Schweigen" ("gentle silence"), both of which contrast
strikingly with the violent movement and the noise of the war
images (as well as with the screams of the disciples two lines
later). From the Last Supper we move—again by association—to
two other scenes described in the Gospels. But these no longer
seem emblematic: they are, in fact, as mimetically "real" as the
war images. The conspicuous metrical straining in the ninth
line—"Náchts schréin . . ."—suggests both the reality of the
biblical scene and the intensity of suffering which the scene
depicts. The suffering of the disciples both parallels and contrasts
with the sufferings of war enacted in the earlier lines: from
one point of view all sufferings are equally horrible; from
another, the sufferings of war must remain meaningless while
those of the disciples are simply a moment in a larger drama
whose positive meanings have been suggested in the image of
the sacrament.

The ambiguities latent within this image of the screaming
disciples are surpassed by those of the final line, with its starkly
visual image of "doubting Thomas" testing the reality of the
resurrected Christ (John 20:24-31). The sense of surprise we
feel when we come to this line is due both to the quietness of
Thomas' gesture, which contrasts with the stridency of the
preceding line, and to the strange discrepancy we feel between
the smallness of the gesture and its largeness of meaning. The
sudden shift from screaming to the recognition of Christ's divinity
suggests, moreover, the mysterious kinship between suffering and
grace. The scar which Thomas touches reveals at once the reality
of Christ's sufferings and the reality of his resurrection; the
positive and negative meanings of suffering are thus once again
fused into a single image. Thomas' act of verification, in addition,
suggests the difficulty of trying to render the meaning of suffering
by means of poetry. Whereas Thomas could experience this
meaning through his sense of touch, the reader of the poem
must, through the very nature of poetry, stand at a remove from
the scenes which the poet portrays. Yet the fact that Thomas
could verify the existence of Christ's scar serves as a guarantee
that the sufferings of modern war can be verified and thus made
comprehensible by means of words; the poet is, in effect, daring
the reader to believe what he has revealed to him.

CHAPTER 3

The Discovery of a Style:
Poems of Late 1912 and Early 1913

I "Psalm"

IF Trakl had stopped writing in mid-1912, such poems as "Die schöne Stadt" and "Menschliches Elend" would have assured him a permanent, though minor, place in the history of German literature. His stature today would be akin to that of his contemporaries Georg Heym and Ernst Stadler, each of whom, like the early Trakl, developed a recognizable voice of his own and a definable, if somewhat narrow, way of apprehending the world. At some time late in 1912, however, Trakl's writing entered a new phase, characterized by radical stylistic experimentation which, in turn, enabled him to explore and define a mode of visionary experience which he had only hinted at in his earlier work.

The transition to this new mode is marked by the poem "Psalm," which is not only longer than any of his earlier poems but is his first attempt at free verse since his unsuccessful early experiments with this form. "Psalm" has many of the features that characterize a poet's transitional work. It extends themes from his earlier work—notably through its images of hospitals and sickness—yet is also full of literary echoes that are not completely assimilated. It tries out a new tone of voice but is unable to modulate this tone with the subtlety of the later poems. It does not, for one thing, know quite where to stop. Moreover, although it contains some very memorable lines and images, it has others which seem awkward and even embarrassing. I quote the first half of the poem:

> Es ist ein Licht, das der Wind ausgelöscht hat.
> Es ist ein Heidekrug, den am Nachmittag ein Betrunkener
>   verlässt.

Es ist ein Weinberg, verbrannt und schwarz mit Löchern
      voll Spinnen.
Es ist ein Raum, den sie mit Milch getüncht haben.
Der Wahnsinnige ist gestorben. Es ist eine Insel der Südsee,
Den Sonnengott zu empfangen. Man rührt die Trommeln.
Die Männer führen kriegerische Tänze auf.
Die Frauen wiegen die Hüften in Schlinggewächsen und
      Feuerblumen,
Wenn das Meer singt. O unser verlorenes Paradies.

Die Nymphen haben die goldenen Wälder verlassen.
Man begräbt den Fremden. Dann hebt ein Flimmerregen an.
Der Sohn des Pan erscheint in Gestalt eines Erdarbeiters,
Der den Mittag am glühenden Asphalt verschläft.
Es sind kleine Mädchen in einem Hof in Kleidchen voll
      herzzerreissender Armut!
Es sind Zimmer, erfüllt von Akkorden und Sonaten.
Es sind Schatten, die sich vor einem erblindeten Spiegel
      umarmen.
An den Fenstern des Spitals wärmen sich Genesende.
Ein weisser Dampfer am Kanal trägt blutige Seuchen herauf.

1   It is a light which the wind has extinguished.
2   It is a village inn which a drunken man leaves behind
       in the afternoon.
3   It is a vineyard, scorched and black with holes full
       of spiders.
4   It is a room which they whitewashed with milk.
5   The madman has died. It is an island in the South Seas
6   Which is to receive the sun-god. The drums are beating.
7   The men perform warlike dances.
8   The women shake their hips among vines and poppies
       [flowers of fire]
9   When the sea sings. O our lost paradise.

10   The nymphs have left the golden forests.
11   They bury the stranger. Then a flickering rain begins.
12   The son of Pan appears in the shape of a ditch-digger
13   Who sleeps away the noon hour on the burning asphalt.
14   It is small girls in a courtyard in dresses full of
        heartrending poverty!
15   It is rooms filled with chords and sonatas.
16   It is shadows which embrace one another before a
        mirror grown blind.

17   In the hospital windows convalescents warm themselves.
18   A white steamer in the canal carries up bloody
       epidemics.

(I, 55)

Like many of the rhymed poems which preceded it, "Psalm"
consists of a series of apparently unconnected images. Yet Trakl
no longer attempts the "merry-go-round" effects which we noted
in the rhymed quatrains of the earlier poems. In several rhymed
poems with six-stress lines contemporaneous with "Psalm"—for
instance, "Drei Blicke in einen Opal" ("Three Glances into an
Opal" [I, 66-67])—one notes a deliberate slowing down, as
though Trakl wanted to give the reader a more protracted view
of the random images he was displaying line after line. But the
long free-verse lines of "Psalm" move even more slowly than
the six-stress lines; indeed, none of his later poems was to utilize
such consistently long lines as these. Syntactically, the poem is
composed largely of two kinds of sentences—those that begin
with the phrase "It is a . . ." and those that present a series of
parallel actions through a subject and verb followed by an
object or adverb. Despite some syntactical variations here and
there, the total effect of the poem is rather monotonous. But
despite its inherent monotony, Trakl's method has also allowed
him to bring together images drawn from totally unrelated
areas of experience into a single context. Mythological beings—
Pan and the nymphs—share a world with convalescents in hospitals. Exotic South Sea vegetation is juxtaposed with a scorched
vineyard. Scarcely defined actions ("They bury the stranger")
alternate with the most concrete scenes ("The women shake
their hips among vines and poppies"). This ability to fuse
together the most diverse phenomena, though sometimes awk-
wardly handled in "Psalm," is to become one of the most conspicuous features of Trakl's major verse.

But "Psalm" also anticipates another central aspect of Trakl's
later work. Despite the diversity of images within the poem,
one is even more strongly aware than in his earlier poetry of
two general areas of imagery which shape the poem: on one
side, "idyllic" images—sounds of music and the "lost paradise"
of a South Sea island—and on the other, images of desolation.
A sense of desolation, indeed, dominates the poem as a whole,
perhaps more fully so in the final half than in the stanzas quoted
above. In historical terms, one could speak of "Psalm" as a

typical early twentieth-century "wasteland" poem; its parallels with Eliot's famous poem of the following decade are by no means exhausted through the image they hold in common of the nymphs who have departed from the modern world.

Yet the contrast between idyllic and desolate states has not been worked out in "Psalm" with the drama and subtlety that characterize this conflict in Trakl's subsequent work. The poem, in fact, has little real development. Except for the first stanza, with its detailed description of the lost South Sea paradise, we find only a random dispersal of images centering about the same theme. Not until the final line, "Schweigsam über der Schädel-stätte öffnen sich Gottes goldene Augen" ("Silently, above the place of skulls [Golgotha], God's golden eyes are opened"), are we aware of any larger framework through which we can view and interpret the events depicted. Here, with the intro-duction of an eternal realm behind all earthly things, the seemingly random images are placed within a single, all-encompassing perspective. Trakl creates this perspective not only through his allusion to Golgotha and the notion of God's presence in the scene but also on the most literal, visual level through the image of the "golden eyes" which silently survey the bleak panorama all around. Yet these allusions to a higher reality scarcely work to undo the general effect of desolation with which the poem is shot through. God remains at best a distant observer, a *deus absconditus*, establishing no contact with the scene below, except, perhaps, by way of some sort of passive, vicarious suffering.

As an experiment in free verse, "Psalm" is significant not only in Trakl's own development but in the development of modern German poetry as a whole. Among all the Western literatures, German has doubtless had the longest history of successful ex-perimentation in nonmetrical, unrhymed verse. Starting with Klopstock in the mid-eighteenth century, most of the major German poets—Goethe, Hölderlin, Novalis, Heine, Mörike, among many others—have contributed distinguished examples in this form. But the free verse of "Psalm" differs as strikingly from these examples as it does from Trakl's juvenile free-verse at-tempts, which were themselves easily identifiable imitations of the earlier German poets. What separates the form and tone of "Psalm" from that of its predecessors is its apparent objectivity, its quiet concentration on unconnected external objects, and its

virtual refusal to let the poet's self intrude. By contrast, in
earlier German free verse—in Goethe's "Prometheus," for example,
or in Hölderlin's late hymns—the illusion of metrical freedom
becomes the occasion for personal monologue, for recording
the questions, assertions, and exhortations of a single, all-
pervading consciousness. In the decade or two preceding "Psalm"
there were, of course, some well-known attempts to create a
new type of free verse, most notably, perhaps, that of the
Naturalist writer Arno Holz in his *Phantasus* of the 1890's, and
that of August Stramm, a Berlin postal clerk who, under the
impact of Marinetti's Futurism, in 1910 began composing lyrics
which radically broke down the conventions of syntax. Today,
the free verse of men such as Holz and Stramm, despite a certain
fascination they may still arouse, seems essentially a dead-end
experimentation without any significant effect on the mainstream
of modern poetry and without sufficient durability in its own
right to seem of more than antiquarian interest.

Trakl's free verse, at least in its initial phase, looks outside
Germany for its impetus. The parallel syntactical constructions,
which in "Psalm" take the place of the metrical regularity of
Trakl's earlier work, would seem to betray the influence of Walt
Whitman, whose poetry was well known in Germany at the turn
of the century and who is one of the relatively few foreign poets
Trakl is known to have mentioned.[1] But the central formative
influence on "Psalm"—as well as on Trakl's poems of the next
few months—was without doubt Arthur Rimbaud.[2] Even if
there were no evidence of influence, the parallels between the
two poets would seem particularly noteworthy in the history of
modern literature. Both came from respectable provincial families, and both rebelled against their middle-class background.
In their addiction to drugs, their sexual deviations (homosexual-
ity in one case, incest in the other) and their inability to feel
at home even in the literary community, their lives are obvious
models of the *poète maudit*. Both experimented in new poetic
forms and succeeded in creating a type of visionary poetry
unique in their respective literatures. Both, moreover, experienced
a short, intense period of creative activity followed by a sudden
break—which for Trakl took the form of suicide; for Rimbaud,
the abandonment of literature. That Trakl felt a strong affinity
with Rimbaud is suggested by his desire, expressed in a letter
of 1912, to travel to Borneo (where Rimbaud was long reputed

to have gone) to "unburden myself of the thunder gathering within me" (I, 488).

Rimbaud's significance in Trakl's literary development was principally that of a catalyst. And it was Rimbaud's example (largely through *Illuminations* and *Une Saison en Enfer* [*A Season in Hell*]) which inspired Trakl to develop a type of free verse new to German literature—a free verse without explicit rhetorical connectives, and one directed to dramatizing the processes of consciousness by means of concrete images rather than by comments *upon* these processes. Indeed, it was through Rimbaud's impact on Trakl that one of the central tendencies of French Symbolism—the conception that a poem makes its statement not by direct pronouncements but through the suggestive power of objects as they are set next to one another—entered the mainstream of German poetry. When Rilke praised Trakl for his contribution to "the liberation of the poetic figure," he referred precisely to the type of innovation which Trakl had derived from Rimbaud.[3]

What little we know of Trakl's development during this crucial period can be pieced together only by internal evidence within the poems themselves. Unlike Ezra Pound, who was steering Anglo-American poetry in a "Symbolist" direction at precisely the same time, Trakl issued no manifestos, nor do his letters provide significant clues to the technical problems with which he was obviously wrestling. One can reconstruct Trakl's development at this point only by means of old-fashioned source hunting. Thus, a comparison of "Psalm" with Rimbaud's prose poem "Enfance" ("Childhood") shows that Trakl derived not only his South Sea images from the French poet but even the syntactical form of his opening lines, which grew out of the following lines of Rimbaud:

> It is a clock which does not toll.
> It is a bog with a nest of white animals.
> It is a cathedral which sinks and a lake that comes up.
> It is a small carriage abandoned in the underbrush, or
>   which goes running down the path
>   decked with ribbons.
> It is a troop of small actors in costumes, seen on the
>   way across the edge of the wood.[4]

A passage such as this one suggests the kind of visionary freedom which Trakl must have sensed in Rimbaud's work and

which, in turn, was to determine the direction of his own
poetry. The poet moves at will from clock to bog to actors
without indicating the connections between these phenomena.
The unreal and the real—the sinking cathedral and the abandoned carriage—can be viewed unselfconsciously within the
same range of vision. Two alternatives which cannot logically
coexist in reality—the carriage which is both abandoned in
the underbrush and which runs down the path—exist side by
side within the poem.

It is noteworthy, moreover, that so relatively untranslatable
a poet as Rimbaud reached Trakl not in the original French
but by way of a pedestrian German translation. Although Trakl
had learned French as a child, he depended largely on a version
of Rimbaud's poems by an Austrian army officer, K. L. Ammer
(whose real name was the very prosaic Karl Klammer, the
last name meaning "clamp" in German).[5] Ammer was an inde-
fatigable translator of French poetry whose versions of Maeterlinck's poems and plays had already influenced Trakl's early
work. The influence of Ammer's Rimbaud, moreover, can be
seen in numerous verbal echoes in Trakl's rhymed poems of
1911-12, but it was not until "Psalm" and his next major poem,
"Helian," that Rimbaud's innovations in poetic language and
structure were to manifest themselves within Trakl's poetry in
their full force. Yet many relatively inconspicuous words and
phrases in Ammer—for instance "sanfter Wahnsinn ("gentle
madness") from Rimbaud's poem on Ophelia's death (Ammer,
p. 138), or "Gottes Wind" ("God's wind") and "Reinheit"
("purity") from *Une Saison en Enfer* (pp. 202, 211)—were to
be echoed time and again by Trakl and to become rich concepts
out of which he could create his own private world of images.
Occasional exclamations in Ammer, such as "O wie traurig, diese
Stunden" ("O how sad these hours" [p. 221]), from "Enfance,"
were to help provide a characteristic rhythm in Trakl's work,
which interrupts long passages of impersonal, descriptive observation with sudden, dramatic exclamations (note, for instance,
the line "O our lost paradise" [l. 9] in "Psalm"). Besides Rimbaud, there were of course other writers, most notably Hölderlin and Dostoevsky, who contributed, in varying ways, to Trakl's
development, but it was above all Rimbaud's mediation which
made Trakl the characteristically modern poet that he is.

II *"Helian"*

The full flowering of Trakl's free-verse manner occurs in "Helian" (written in December, 1912, and January, 1913), one of his most celebrated and difficult poems and, at the same time, the poem which contains the most numerous echoes from Ammer's Rimbaud translations. "Helian," together with those of Rilke's *Duino Elegies* that date back to 1912, is probably the first major poem in German written in an uncompromisingly Symbolist style. From beginning to end one senses the vitality that accompanies the discovery of a new way of expression. The poem's essential manner—its imagery, tone, syntax, progressions, its mode of organization—is more or less representative of the remainder of Trakl's work. Although it is his longest poem in verse—two of his later prose poems and an early version of another poem exceed it in length—I quote it in full (I have added section numbers for the reader's convenience):

I

In den einsamen Stunden des Geistes
Ist es schön, in der Sonne zu gehn
An den gelben Mauern des Sommers hin.
Leise klingen die Schritte im Gras; doch immer schläft
Der Sohn des Pan im grauen Marmor.

Abends auf der Terrasse betranken wir uns mit braunem
      Wein.
Rötlich glüht der Pfirsich im Laub;
Sanfte Sonate, frohes Lachen.

Schön ist die Stille der Nacht.
Auf dunklem Plan
Begegnen wir uns mit Hirten und weissen Sternen.

Wenn es Herbst geworden ist
Zeigt sich nüchterne Klarheit im Hain.
Besänftigte wandeln wir an roten Mauern hin
Und die runden Augen folgen dem Flug der Vögel.
Am Abend sinkt das weisse Wasser in Graburnen.

In kahlen Gezweigen feiert der Himmel.
In reinen Händen trägt der Landmann Brot and Wein
Und friedlich reifen die Früchte in sonniger Kammer.

O wie ernst ist das Antlitz der teueren Toten.
Doch die Seele erfreut gerechtes Anschaun.

II

Gewaltig ist das Schweigen des verwüsteten Gartens,
Da der junge Novize die Stirne mit braunem Laub bekränzt,
Sein Odem eisiges Gold trinkt.

Die Hände rühren das Alter bläulicher Wasser
Oder in kalter Nacht die weissen Wangen der Schwestern.

Leise und harmonisch ist ein Gang an freundlichen Zimmern
            hin,
Wo Einsamkeit ist und das Rauschen des Ahorns,
Wo vielleicht noch die Drossel singt.

Schön ist der Mensch und erscheinend im Dunkel,
Wenn er staunend Arme und Beine bewegt,
Und in purpurnen Höhlen stille die Augen rollen.

Zur Vesper verliert sich der Fremdling in schwarzer
            Novemberzerstörung,
Unter morschem Geäst, an Mauern voll Aussatz hin,
Wo vordem der heilige Bruder gegangen,
Versunken in das sanfte Saitenspiel seines Wahnsinns,

O wie einsam endet der Abendwind.
Ersterbend neigt sich das Haupt im Dunkel des Ölbaums.

III

Erschütternd ist der Untergang des Geschlechts.
In dieser Stunde füllen sich die Augen des Schauenden
Mit dem Gold seiner Sterne.

Am Abend versinkt ein Glockenspiel, das nicht mehr tönt,
Verfallen die schwarzen Mauern am Platz,
Ruft der tote Soldat zum Gebet.

Ein bleicher Engel
Tritt der Sohn ins leere Haus seiner Väter.

Die Schwestern sind ferne zu weissen Greisen gegangen.
Nachts fand sie der Schläfer unter den Säulen im Hausflur,
Zurückgekehrt von traurigen Pilgerschaften.

O wie starrt von Kot und Würmern ihr Haar,
Da er darein mit silbernen Füssen steht,
Und jene verstorben aus kahlen Zimmern treten.

O ihr Psalmen in feurigen Mitternachtsregen,
Da die Knechte mit Nesseln die sanften Augen schlugen,
Die kindlichen Früchte des Hollunders
Sich staunend neigen über ein leeres Grab.

Leise rollen vergilbte Monde
Über die Fieberlinnen des Jünglings,
Eh dem Schweigen des Winters folgt.

IV

Ein erhabenes Schicksal sinnt den Kidron hinab,
Wo die Zeder, ein weiches Geschöpf,
Sich unter den blauen Brauen des Vaters entfaltet,
Über die Weide nachts ein Schäfer seine Herde führt.
Oder es sind Schreie im Schlaf,
Wenn ein eherner Engel im Hain den Menschen antritt,
Das Fleisch des Heiligen auf glühendem Rost hinschmilzt.

Um die Lehmhütten rankt purpurner Wein,
Tönende Bündel vergilbten Korns,
Das Summen der Bienen, der Flug des Kranichs.
Am Abend begegnen sich Auferstandene auf Felsenpfaden.

In schwarzen Wassern spiegeln sich Aussätzige;
Oder sie öffnen die kotbefleckten Gewänder
Weinend dem balsamischen Wind, der vom rosigen Hügel
          weht.

Schlanke Mägde tasten durch die Gassen der Nacht,
Ob sie den liebenden Hirten fänden.
Sonnabends tönt in den Hütten sanfter Gesang.

Lasset das Lied auch des Knaben gedenken,
Seines Wahnsinns, und weisser Brauen und seines Hingangs,
Des Verwesten, der bläulich die Augen aufschlägt.
O wie traurig ist dieses Wiedersehn.

V

Die Stufen des Wahnsinns in schwarzen Zimmern,
Die Schatten der Alten unter der offenen Tür,

Da Helians Seele sich im rosigen Spiegel beschaut
Und Schnee und Aussatz von seiner Stirne sinken.

An den Wänden sind die Sterne erloschen
Und die weissen Gestalten des Lichts.

Dem Teppich entsteigt Gebein der Gräber,
Das Schweigen verfallener Kreuze am Hügel,
Des Weihrauchs Süsse im purpurnen Nachtwind.

O ihr zerbrochenen Augen in schwarzen Mündern,
Da der Enkel in sanfter Umnachtung
Einsam dem dunkleren Ende nachsinnt,
Der stille Gott die blauen Lider über ihn senkt.

I

1   In the lonely hours of the spirit
2   It is beautiful to walk in the sun
3   Along the yellow walls of summer.
4   Softly the steps sound in the grass; but always
5   The son of Pan sleeps in the gray marble.

6   In the evening, on the terrace, we got [used to get]
       drunk on brown wine.
7   The peach glows reddish in the leaves;
8   Soft sonata, joyous laughter.

9   Beautiful is the stillness of night.
10   On a dark plain
11   We meet shepherds and white stars.

12   When it has turned autumn,
13   Sober clarity emerges in the grove.
14   Calmed, we stroll along red walls
15   And the [our] round eyes follow the birds' flight.
16   In the evening the white water sinks in sepulchral urns.

17   In bare branches the sky is resting [celebrates].
18   In clean hands the peasant carries bread and wine
19   And the fruits ripen peacefully in [a] sunny room.

20   Oh how solemn is the face of the beloved dead.
21   Yet the soul delights in righteous contemplation.

II

22 Mighty is the silence of the devastated garden,
23 When the young novice wreathes his forehead with
        brown leaves,
24 [When] his breath drinks icy gold.

25 The hands touch the old age of bluish waters
26 Or, in [a] cold night, the white cheeks of the sisters.

27 Quiet and harmonious is a walk past friendly rooms,
28 Where there is solitude and the maple's rustling,
29 Where the thrush perhaps still sings.

30 Beautiful is man and appearing [shining, like an
        apparition] in the darkness,
31 When, amazed, he moves his arms and legs,
32 And his eyes roll quietly in purple sockets.

33 At vespers the stranger loses himself in black November-
        destruction,
34 Under rotten branches, along walls full of leprosy,
35 Where the holy brother had gone earlier,
36 Immersed in the soft string music of his madness.

37 Oh how lonely the evening wind ends.
38 Dying away [by degrees], the head bends down in
        the dark of the olive tree.

III

39 Overwhelming is the fall of the race [family].
40 At this hour the eyes of the beholder are filled
41 With the gold of his stars.

42 In the evening, bells which no longer ring sink down,
43 The black walls in the square fall into ruins,
44 The dead soldier calls to prayer.

45 A pale angel,
46 The son steps into the empty house of his fathers.

47 The sisters have gone far away to white old men.
48 At night the sleeper found them under the columns
        in the entrance hall,
49 Returned from sad pilgrimages.

50   Oh how their hair bristles with muck and worms,
51   When he steps into it with silver feet,
52   And they, having died, step out of bare rooms.

53   Oh, ye psalms in fiery midnight rains,
54   When the servants smote their gentle eyes with nettles
55   [When] the childlike fruits of the elderberry
56   Bend down astonished over an empty grave.

57   Softly, yellowed moons roll
58   Over the youth's fever sheets,
59   Before the silence of winter comes.

IV

60   A sublime fate meditates down the Kidron,
61   Where the cedar, a soft creature,
62   Unfolds under the blue brows of the father.
63   Over the meadow at night a shepherd leads his flock.
64   Or there are screams in sleep,
65   When a brazen angel approaches [the] man in the
         grove,
66   [When] the saint's flesh melts away on a blazing grate.

67   Around the mud-huts purple vines climb,
68   Resounding sheaves of yellowed grain,
69   The humming of the bees, the flight of the crane.
70   In the evening [the] resurrected meet on rocky paths.

71   Lepers cast their reflections in black waters;
72   Or they open their muck-spattered robes
73   Weeping to the fragrant [balmy] wind which blows
         from the rosy hill.

74   Slim maids grope through the alleyways of the night,
75   That they might find the loving shepherd.
76   On Saturdays gentle singing is heard in the huts.

77   Let the song commemorate also the boy,
78   His madness, and [his] white brows and his death
         [departing],
79   The decayed [one], who bluishly opens his eyes.
80   Oh how sad is this reunion.

V

81   The stages [steps] of madness in black rooms,
82   The shadows of the aged under the open door,

83 When Helian's soul looks at itself in the rosy mirror
84 And snow and leprosy sink from his forehead.

85 On the walls the stars are extinguished
86 And the white figures of the light.

87 Skeletons from the graves rise out of the carpet,
88 The silence of decayed crosses on the hill,
89 The sweetness of the incense in the purple night wind.

90 Oh you shattered eyes in black mouths,
91 When the grandson in gentle madness [be-nightedness]
92 In solitude reflects upon the darker end,
93 [When] the silent god lowers his blue eyelids over him.

                                                    (I, 69-73)

Most attempts to interpret "Helian" have come to nought through the insistence of critics to read the poem as though it were an example either of Christian allegory or of what the Germans call *Erlebnislyrik*, poetry describing the author's "experience."[6] In all too many instances, Trakl's critics have failed to take into account the poem's Symbolist background and, instead, have approached it with much the same critical technique as they would use, say, to analyze a Goethe lyric or a nineteenth-century novel. Thus, they would search through the poem for a meaningful sequence of events which could be related, in one way or another, to Trakl's life or to Christian religious experience. Yet the poem, by its nature, resists such a method. As an alternative, I shall start with what may seem random and even trivial observations on its language and organization and only later speculate on what the poem is trying to say.

Perhaps the most conspicuous feature of "Helian's" style, compared to that of "Psalm" and the poems in rhyme, is the absence of neatly parallel rows of images. The earlier work, like "Helian," was, of course, characterized by a lack of abstractions and a corresponding dependence on concrete images and miniature dramatic situations. But the monotony that marred much of this earlier work is no longer present. Quite in contrast, the verse of "Helian" has a suppleness which Trakl never before achieved. Consider the second stanza:

Abends auf der Terrasse betranken wir uns mit braunem Wein.
Rötlich glüht der Pfirsich im Laub;
Sanfte Sonate, frohes Lachen.

> In the evening, on the terrace, we got [used to
>   get] drunk on brown wine.
> The peach glows reddish in the leaves;
> Soft sonata, joyous laughter.

Each line is not only varied in its length and its syntax, but each successively portrays a different mode of perception. The first line, which is in the first person and past tense, recites a memory, though the narrative of which it is presumably a part is never actually developed or even sketched in. The second line, through its shift to the present tense and the third person, seems, superficially at least, unrelated to the preceding line; it attempts, moreover, to describe a visual object in all its immediacy. The third line contains no verb but merely lists two auditory phenomena, each qualified by an adjective.

Trakl's technique of employing undeveloped dramatic situations is what Yvor Winters aptly, though also disparagingly, calls "pseudo-reference" in describing the manner of such modern American poets working in the Symbolist tradition as Hart Crane and T. S. Eliot.[7] In the poetry written in this tradition, it is irrelevant and even misleading for the reader to ask himself such traditional questions as "What is the setting of this poem?" or "Who are these characters?" or "Where did they come from, and how are they going to be developed?" Not only in this stanza from "Helian," but throughout the poem, we find constant shifts in scene, with changes from tense to tense and person to person. Sometimes, when a sudden imperative is introduced, as in line 77—"Let the song commemorate also the boy"—it seems as though a new voice had intruded from nowhere. Characters and places—the sisters, the Kidron River, even Helian himself—are familiarly alluded to without previous identification; and in the frequent breaks between stanzas we sense the presence of mysterious, unexpressed events, or, to use the metaphor applied by Rilke in his remarks on "Helian," "large, unpossessable plains" that are, as it were, "fenced off" by the short stanzas.[8] Like *The Waste Land,* with which it shares a common Symbolist heritage, "Helian" gives the impression of being a longer, vaster, more comprehensive poem than its actual length indicates.

The shifts in syntax and point of view which create this impression of mysterious depth are paralleled by subtle metrical changes absent from Trakl's earlier poems. The poems in rhyme are, in fact, notable for their lack of metrical variation; and

"Psalm," with its largely iambic pattern throughout, manifests as much metrical as syntactical monotony. The constant metrical variations of "Helian," however, represent both a break with the past and a new metrical mode typical of nearly all of Trakl's later free verse. The poem's first stanza, for instance, might be scanned as follows:

> x x / x x / x x / x
> In den einsamen Stunden des Geistes
> x x / x x / x x /
> Ist es schön, in der Sonne zu gehn
> x x / x / x x / x /
> An den gelben Mauern des Sommers hin.
> / x / x x / x x / x / x /
> Leise klingen die Schritte im Gras; doch immer schläft
> x / x / x / x / x
> Der Sohn des Pan im grauen Marmor.

I have not indicated half-accents, though the first word of each of the first two lines should probably be read this way.[9] I am trying to show, rather, that in these three opening lines Trakl sets up what seems to be a recurrent pattern, soon starts to vary it, and then suddenly changes to a new pattern altogether. If we count the first word of the first three lines as unstressed, each of the first two lines consists of anapests. Yet despite this recurrent pattern, the lines differ from one another through the addition of a feminine ending in the first line and the internal half-rhyme ("schön"-"gehn") in the second. A more marked variation occurs in the third line, which consists of only two anapests, the other two feet each having one less unaccented syllable.

With the fourth line, an entirely new pattern is initiated. Up to now, the speaker has been musing to himself. Now, as he describes a specific event, and one that occurs in the immediate present, he shifts to a falling rhythm, a trochee followed by two dactyls. This line, like many others in Trakl's free verse, could almost be a hexameter—but only up to the caesura, after which he shifts to an iambic pattern, which, in turn, he maintains throughout the last line of the stanza. This shift again accompanies a new direction in thought: "doch immer" ("but always"), he announces, changing from the description of a single event to a type of reflection encompassing both past and present. One could summarize thus: Trakl will seem to establish a metrical pattern, only to alter it as soon as the reader becomes aware of it. The variations are sometimes gradual, as in the first three lines, and sometimes sudden, as in the fourth line; yet they are nearly always tied to shifts in imagery, syntax, and idea. It is an infinitely subtle music, patterned yet changing, a music fully suited to the breadth of vision toward which the poem as a whole is reaching.

Among the many fragments of plot in "Helian," can one at least discern a central narrative, or some meaningful line of development? In one sense, yes. If one seeks to isolate the predominant imagery in each section, one can make out a narrative of sorts, one that moves from processes of decay to hints of rebirth and resurrection. Thus, the first section can be described as a movement from relatively "positive" images (marble statuary, wine drinking on the terrace—the sort of images that predominate in earlier poems such as "Die schöne Stadt") to images of simple country life in autumn, a time of increasing barrenness, a time, moreover, that suggests the imminent death of nature. The second section presents scenes of increasing decay and devastation within what seems to be a monastic setting. The third section intensifies these images, but the predominant setting is now the fallen world of the family household, with its various inhabitants going to their doom in different ways. Christian imagery dominates the fourth section. Much of it is pastoral in nature, a New Testament world of lepers, herds, and cedars, with intimations of resurrection. The short concluding section recapitulates images—madness, resurrection, decay—from earlier passages of the poem, but the resolution remains ambiguous. The poem's protagonist is cleansed of his leprosy and even seems to be blessed by God in the final line, but at the same time he contemplates a "darker end." It would be tempting to speak of a Christian death-and-rebirth pattern shaping the poem. Yet the problematic quality of the conclusion makes it difficult to postulate any single pattern unequivocally.[10]

The reader who wishes to chart the poem as a whole is perhaps on safer ground if, rather than generalizing on the "meaning" of each section, he starts with specific images and traces them through the poem. One could take the various allusions to the seasons, for instance. The first section moves from late summer into fall; the second, with its gradually increasing images of decay, mentions "November-destruction" (the word is typical of the compounds which, after "Helian," become more and more frequent in Trakl's work.) The third section ends with an allusion to winter, but the two remaining ones contain no specific seasonal references, unless one interprets the "fragrant wind" in the fourth part as a sign of spring. References to wind move from the lonely "evening wind" at the end of the second section through the "fragrant wind" and finally to the purple "night wind" of the final section. Images of leprosy, in turn, shift from the "walls full of leprosy" (34), to the lepers casting reflections in black waters (71), and finally to the shedding of the leprous scabs from Helian's forehead (84).

All of these images would surely support a theory about "Helian" as a poem of death and regeneration. Still, despite the indubitable presence of this pattern in the poem, there are other patterns against which it must be measured. If, in one sense, the poem moves gradually toward death and then toward rebirth, in another sense it moves back and forth from moment to moment between positive and negative aspects of reality. This second pattern is not as clearly discernible in "Helian" as it is in some of Trakl's later poems, for example in "Elis," which I shall take up in the next chapter. Yet throughout Trakl's verse, as I have already indicated, one can distinguish between two sharply contrasting visions of the world, the one characterized by images of decay and dissolution (images that are sometimes of a distinctly demonic nature), the other by pastoral landscapes and images of a once idyllic past. In the third section of "Helian," to give one example, directly after the graphic description of the sisters with "muck and worms in their hair," Trakl introduces the "childlike fruits of the elderberry." Again, at the beginning of the fourth section, after the benign images of the cedar and the shepherd and his flock, an antithetical vision suddenly intrudes with the line, "Or there are screams in sleep." These are relatively conspicuous examples of Trakl's use of alternations. Yet throughout the poem the reader is aware of subtle qualifications which serve to undermine any generalizations he is tempted to make about the poem's themes and progressions. The word "sanft" (meaning "soft," "gentle," "mild") is used at crucial spots —in lines 36 and 91, for instance—to qualify images of madness and decay. Indeed, the statements the poem purports to be making are so modified throughout that the ambiguousness of

Trakl's utterances must be recognized as a major aspect of his theme.

The ambiguousness which informs the central "narrative" is reflected in the uncertainties which mark the attempts of critics to identify and describe the poem's protagonist. Where did Trakl derive the name Helian? Why is Helian named directly only in the final section? To what degree is the protagonist an example of self-portraiture? The title's source has been identified variously as the Old High German poem *Heliand* (which Trakl may not even have remembered from his school days); "Heiland" (German for "Savior"); "Helios" (the sun image runs through the poem); and "Lélian," a name which Verlaine applied to himself in his self-portrait in *Les Poètes Maudits* (*The Cursed Poets*). One critic has suggested a fusion of Helios and Lélian, which would bring together two extreme conceptions of the modern poet, who can thus be seen at once as cosmic creativity and suffering *poète maudit*.[11] Both extremes are in keeping with the spirit of the poem; I, for one, would just as soon throw in "Heiland" as a plausible analogue.

If Helian does not appear by name until the final section, he appears in various guises or "aspects" throughout the poem. He is the youth in "fever linens"; the son who enters his empty ancestral home; the young novice; the "decayed" one; the stranger; the mad boy; perhaps also the holy brother, the loving shepherd, and the saint on the hot grill. What matters, however, is not that these figures are meant to be "identical" with Helian, but rather that Trakl has chosen to fragment his protagonist among a large number of guises. To put it another way: there is no single protagonist or central character, at least not in the conventional literary sense; instead there is a group of analogous figures—some of them benign, others afflicted with death and dissolution—who are dispersed throughout the poem in accordance with the alternating visions of death and decay.

To speak of Helian as an example of self-portraiture, as some of Trakl's critics have done, is to put the question the wrong way. In one sense, of course, we can speak of Helian, as well as such figures in later poems as Elis, Sebastian, Kaspar Hauser, and the many unnamed wanderers, strangers, and dead men, as "masks" through which Trakl speaks or reflects aspects of himself. Such an observation, however, seems less relevant than one which would approach the poem from the opposite direction: it is remarkable, one could assert,, how thoroughly Trakl manages to distance himself from the "characters" of the poem. The central fact about the protagonist is not that he is a monk or a savior or even a corpse but rather that he is fragmented into many beings at once. These beings exist as though in a dream, within a dreamer's mind, one might say, yet they remain strangely independent of him; it is as if the poet could portray himself only by fragmenting himself and projecting the fragments as far distantly as possible. If anything, Trakl's mature verse shows an extreme reticence to engage in overtly personal utterance; like other poetry in the Symbolist tradition, it deliberately rejects the Romantic convention that a poem is the overt expression of the writer's personal experience.

This is not to say that "Helian" is an "impersonal" poem, with no discernible relation to its creator; in some respects, indeed, it is more personal than anything Trakl had written before, but it is personal in a peculiarly modern way. Trakl, we know, was much attached to "Helian" and, in one of the relatively few comments he made on specific poems, spoke of it as "the most precious and painful [poem] I have ever written" (I, 501). Since this comment was made shortly after the poem was written, one can assume that he had now found a way of writing poetry that allowed him to explore the intricacies of the self more fully than any of his earlier poetic modes could do. But if one *must* seek the personal element in "Helian," one would do best not to ask who the protagonist is, and then try to reduce his various guises to their lowest common denominator, but rather to chart the poem's emotional rhythms. By these rhythms I mean, for instance, the alternations between positive and negative states that occur throughout the poem, alternations which could be said to correspond to the sharp changes in emotion which Trakl himself had described in the letter to his sister Minna which I cited in the last chapter.

Beyond the poem's personal dimension, critics have stressed at least two other areas of meaning within "Helian": first, its depiction of the decline of civilization; second, its Christian overtones. The first of these interpretations was voiced initially by Karl Borromäus Heinrich, a fellow member of the *Brenner* circle, who published an article on Trakl in the *Brenner* only one month after the publication of "Helian." In this first critical essay ever written on Trakl, Heinrich not only acknowledged "Helian"

as a major poem but attempted to define it as a kind of prophecy
on the decline of the West:

Through "Helian" I was able to throw a profound glance into the
soul of the poet, whose most profound vision is enacted in "Helian":
as profound as it rightly must be in order to [create] such a poem of
fate, under whose sign its poet was born and the writing of which
was part of his [Trakl's] tragic but lofty mission; a poem which is
a revelation at once of the dying away of the Occident and of the
rich, sinking beauty of its decline [extinction] as could be uttered only
through this poet's mouth; a revelation which, once uttered, however,
belongs to the world forever. For in "Helian" one who has "returned
from sad pilgrimages" [l. 49] has experienced and recorded his
own and his race's [family's] personal fate in so peculiarly European
a manner that every [reader] will be touched by it in his innermost
being: precisely because every European is, in one way or another,
concerned with this fate. Accordingly, the richness of forms which is
revealed in "Helian" extends from the most distant past to the end
of the race; behind [this richness] lies a long intellectual tradition.[12]

Heinrich writes in a now outmoded form of German whose
pretentiousness shows up embarrassingly in translation; yet
he is able to point up a central level of meaning in the poem.
Spenglerism, one can see, was in the air well before *The Decline
of the West* (whose German title *Der Untergang des Abend-
landes* even echoes two words in Heinrich's essay) was published
in 1918.[13] Heinrich's statement, moreover, picks up certain crucial
words from the poem: for instance, "Untergang" ("decline,"
"going downward," "downfall"); "Geschlecht" ("family," "sex,"
"human race"); "versinkende" ("sinking," "foundering," "going
downward"); "Schicksal" ("fate"). Trakl, in turn, was to pick
up at least three words from Heinrich's essay—"das Abendland"
("the Occident," "the land of evening"); "Offenbarung" ("revelation," "prophecy," "laying bare"); and "die Abgeschiedenheit"
(a word drawn from the title of the essay and meaning "solitude," "privacy," "withdrawal," "the state of someone departed
or dead")—and put these to complex use in many of his later
poems, as one sees in such titles as "Abendländisches Lied" ("Oc-
cidental Song" [I, 119]); "Gesang des Abgeschiedenen" ("Song
of the Departed One" [I, 144]); and "Offenbarung und Untergang" ("Revelation and Decline" [I, 168-70]). Here, one might
say, is a notable example of criticism helping to shape poetry;
the vision of history which serves as one layer of meaning in
"Helian" was to become a continually richer concept in Trakl's

later work. Yet what seems to me most significant about the historical vision is that it is only one of *several* layers of meaning. The powerful line which opens the third section, "Erschütternd ist der Untergang des Geschlechts," refers at once to the disintegration of the family (which is pictured in detail in the succeeding lines) and to the decline of the race (both the "European" and the human race). Given Trakl's Symbolist method, which implies the poet's refusal to control his meanings by direct statement, the reader can hold multiple interpretations of this line in his mind at the same time.

Once the Symbolist nature of this poem is understood, one can no longer, as did such Trakl commentators of the 1950's as Eduard Lachmann or the Jesuit critic Alfred Focke, insist on a Christian interpretation of his work.[14] I do not, of course, mean to deny Trakl's own profession of faith. At least one such profession, part of a conversation held in the winter of 1913-14 between Trakl and a Swiss writer, Hans Limbach, has been recorded in detail; yet the mode of Christianity which emerges from Trakl's remarks is a peculiar blend of Kierkegaardian and Dostoevskian ideas characteristic of the *Brenner* circle at this time.[15] Trakl's Christianity, at least as it emerges in his poems, is a distinctly "literary" Christianity, one that is neither doctrinal in intent, like the Christianity of George Herbert's *Temple,* nor a direct confession of faith such as one can find even in so Symbolist a poem as T. S. Eliot's "Ash Wednesday."

Trakl's poems utilize the structure and imagery of Christian experience without, however, committing themselves to a specifically Christian range of meanings. The image of the shepherd and his flock which runs through "Helian" undoubtedly refers, on one level, to Christ and his followers, but at the same time it remains a symbol of a traditional, ordered form of life to contrast with images of decay and disintegration. Christ, one might say, exists here as an analogue, not as the representation of a real figure. It is noteworthy, besides, that the poem's most specifically Christian images—the river Kidron (l. 60), the saint on the grate (l. 66), the sad pilgrimages (l. 49), even the phrase "righteous contemplation" (l. 21)—were drawn by Trakl neither from the Bible nor from saints' legends, but from Ammer's translation of Rimbaud (*see* Ammer, pp. 205, 220, 215).

Moreover, the uncertainty which we noted in the resolution of "Helian"—is the protagonist saved, damned, or what?—is reflected by the uncertainties evident in Trakl's process of composition. As the critical edition indicates, the final line of the poem, in which God seems benignly to lower his eyelids over Helian, was, in an earlier version, followed by three lines which rendered the "reunion" of God and Helian somewhat equivocal:

> . . . jener über zerbrochene Stufen schweigend ins Dunkel
>   hinabsteigt
> unter Weiden ein weisser Wandrer
> durch die nächtige Landschaft seiner Seele.

> he silently descends over broken steps into the dark.
> a white wanderer under willows
> through the nocturnal landscape of his soul.   (II, 132)

As it turned out, Trakl not only discarded these lines from "Helian" but adapted them in varying ways in two short lyrics written about this time (see I, 65, 387). One suspects that he remained uncertain on what note to end the poem until a relatively late stage of composition.

A study of the poem's evolution through its various drafts makes clearer than any critical commentary that Trakl, like his French Symbolist predecessors, was concerned with the suggestive power of images and lines rather than with the exposition of a body of ideas. To take some examples from other poems, at one point Trakl substituted the word "summer-night" for "winter-night" (II, 307); at another point the phrase "the cool head" for its virtual opposite, "the burning head" (II, 226).

In addition, as Walther Killy has demonstrated, "Helian" was probably not at first conceived as an independent entity but emerged gradually out of a series of rough passages, parts of which, like the original closing lines quoted above, were formed into various shorter poems—"Abendlied" ("Evening Song" [I, 65], "Rosenkranzlieder" ("Rosary Songs" [I, 57-58]), "Untergang" ("Decline" [I, 116, 386-89])—which Trakl published soon after "Helian."[16] The unique manner in which all these poems—Killy refers to them as the "'Helian'-complex"—took shape is only one among several indications, then, that "Helian" represents a strikingly new development in the history of German poetry. As such, this poem, as well as Trakl's later poems, all of which are extensions of its basic mode, demands a critical vocabulary and a method of analysis appropriate to the premises on which it is built.

CHAPTER 4

The Language of Process: Poems of 1913

I The Semblance of Myth: the "Elis" Poems

AFTER "Helian," Trakl's development was never again to show the astonishingly rapid growth which took place in late 1912 and early 1913. The work of the last eighteen months of his life was essentially a consolidation of the discoveries he had made in "Helian" and a gradual development of several new forms and tones of voice. If we define the last year and a half in terms of language, we can speak of an increasing degree of stylization and a tendency toward personal mannerism. If we approach it by way of influence, we note a sharply decreasing dependence on Rimbaud and—though no writer was to have a comparable effect—an increased interest in Hölderlin and Dostoevsky. Thematically, the later poems consolidate a private set of images whose traces were discernible from Trakl's earliest work, but whose central terms—a world polarized by idyllic landscapes and images of decay—come more consistently to control the organization of his poems in the period after "Helian." In terms of formal elements, the vast majority of Trakl's remaining poems are free-verse lyrics not radically different, in their total organization or their use of the stanza form, from "Helian" or the shorter lyrics that came out of the so-called "'Helian'-complex."

Yet during this period Trakl also tried out at least three forms which indicate distinctly new directions in his work: first, a new type of rhymed poem (dating from the last half of 1913) which is not only essentially different from the "merry-go-round" poems of 1910-12 but which embodies many of the stylistic and schematic features of his free verse; second, a form of prose poem (of which he composed four examples between late 1913 and mid-1914) which intensifies his essential images and themes within a thicker, more closely crowded texture than was possible in verse; and third, a tense, cryptic

81

form (developed in the spring of 1914) consisting of short lines of free verse that follow one another with a wild, demonic rapidity, in place of the measured slowness of his other poems.

In the present chapter, I shall illustrate these various tendencies in five poems written between "Helian" and early 1914: the two so-called Elis poems, which create the semblance of a private myth; "Am Mönchsberg" ("On the Mönchsberg"), typical of many of the short lyrics in free verse; and two rhymed poems, "Sonja" ("Sonia") and "Ein Winterabend" ("A Winter Evening"), both of which, together with "Am Mönchsberg," appear to represent particular narrative moments in a larger myth. Much of my discussion will center around the nature of this apparent myth and its relevance to the interpretation of individual poems. In the following chapter I shall take up "Traum und Umnachtung" ("Dream and Madness"), which seems to me the greatest of the prose poems; "Das Gewitter" ("The Thunderstorm"), representative of Trakl's swift-moving, short-line poems; and "Grodek" and "Klage" ("Lament"), his last two poems, in which he places his war experience within the framework of his private world of images. I start with "An den Knaben Elis" ("To the Boy Elis"), written in the spring of 1913:

Elis, wenn die Amsel im schwarzen Wald ruft,
Dieses ist dein Untergang.
Deine Lippen trinken die Kühle des blauen Felsenquells.

Lass, wenn deine Stirne leise blutet
Uralte Legenden
Und dunkle Deutung des Vogelflugs.

Du aber gehst mit weichen Schritten in die Nacht,
Die voll purpurner Trauben hängt,
Und du regst die Arme schöner im Blau.

Ein Dornenbusch tönt,
Wo deine mondenen Augen sind.
O, wie lange bist, Elis, du verstorben.

Dein Leib ist eine Hyazinthe,
In die ein Mönch die wächsernen Finger taucht.
Eine schwarze Höhle ist unser Schweigen,

Daraus bisweilen ein sanftes Tier tritt
Und langsam die schweren Lider senkt.
Auf deine Schläfen tropft schwarzer Tau,

Das letzte Gold verfallener Sterne.

1 Elis, when the blackbird calls in the black wood,
2 This is your decline [descent, extinction].
3 Your lips drink the coolness of the blue rock-spring.

4 When your forehead softly bleeds,[1] refrain from
5 Primeval legends
6 And [the] dark interpretation of bird flight.

7 But you walk with soft steps into the night,
8 Which hangs full of purple grapes,
9 And you move your arms more beautifully in the blue.

10 A bramble bush sounds
11 Where your moonlike eyes are.
12 Oh how long, Elis, you have been dead.

13 Your body is a hyacinth,
14 Into which a monk dips his waxen fingers.
15 Our silence is a black cave,

16 From which now and then a gentle animal steps out
17 And slowly lowers its heavy eyelids.
18 On your temples black dew drips,

19 The final gold of ruined [fallen] stars.

(I, 84)

This poem serves as well as any to indicate the features of Trakl's "blue" world, a set of related images which recur persistently in his work after "Helian." The dark forest, rocks, a spring, a gentle animal, a blackbird, purple grapes, quietude, hyacinthian and moonlike things, blueness, night—these are the images typical of the idyllic landscapes which Trakl contrasts with scenes of disintegration. In Trakl's geography, the idyllic is not located "above" the fallen world, as in most earlier poetry, but "below."[2] Yet the idyll which Trakl evokes here and else-where remains something remote both in time and place. Elis is long dead, and the landscape associated with him is at best a precarious one. Images that suggest suffering intrude continually. Thus, a "sounding" bush of thorns—a frequent image in Trakl's poetry, and one which seems to carry overtones of God appearing to Moses in the burning bush—stands juxtaposed with Elis' eyes. The gentle animal lowers his heavy lids as though it were about to die. The gold which illuminates Elis' temples is the "final" gold of stars which have somehow disintegrated. To evoke the world of Elis is at once to evoke its breakdown.

"Who is this Elis?" one is tempted to ask from the start. Considerable scholarly energy has been spent in tracking down Trakl's sources. Elysium and the Peloponnesian region called Elis have both been suggested, but since the mid-1950's Trakl's critics have agreed that he derived the name Elis from Elis Fröbom, a seventeenth-century Swedish miner who fell into a mineshaft on his wedding day and, when his body was retrieved many years later, was found in a perfect state of preservation, with the full appearance of youth, while his betrothed had meanwhile become an aged crone. The subject, with its obvious contrast between a timeless world and the phenomenal world in which men grow old and deteriorate, had been treated several times in German literature before Trakl, most notably by the Romantic writer E. T. A. Hoffmann, in *Die Bergwerke zu Falun* (*The Mines in Falun*, 1818), and by Hugo von Hofmannsthal, whose uncompleted verse drama, *Das Bergwerk von Falun* (*The Mine in Falun*, 1906), Trakl doubtless knew.[3]

A search for detailed parallels between Trakl's poem and these sources is of little use, however, in interpreting the poem, for Trakl customarily used the sources for his "characters" only to suggest an initial idea which he then developed on his own. The blueness of Trakl's nocturnal landscape, for that matter, does not come from either of these literary embodiments of Elis Fröbom's story but was probably suggested by the blue flower of Novalis, to whom Trakl dedicated one of his most exquisite poems ("An Novalis" ["To Novalis"–I, 324-26]). The reader who is eager to find analogies outside the poem might attempt to tie the imagery of this landscape to the visions induced by the various drugs which Trakl regularly used; indeed, Trakl's frequent reference to poppies within this landscape (not in this particular poem, although in numerous others) seems directly to invite such interpretation. From a more distinctly literary point of view, one can treat this imagery as a peculiar version of pastoral which has its roots, if not precisely in rustics and shepherds, at least in the various forms of what Northrop Frye calls the "lower paradise": the earthly paradises of Dante, Spenser, and Milton; Blake's "Beulah-land"; and, of special relevance to Trakl, the imagery of night and under-earthly things to be found in Novalis.[4]

One can even attempt, as I did in my dissertation on Trakl many years ago, to outline a larger narrative of innocence, guilt, and expiation that informs Trakl's mature poetry and of which each poem constitutes a fragment. In retrospect, my attempt seems to me largely unsuccessful, if only because such a "larger narrative" was never consistently worked out either in the poetry or, as far as one can tell, in Trakl's mind. I now prefer to state the problem in the following way: although each of Trakl's poems gives the illusion of being a fragment of a myth, this myth itself must not be thought of in sequential terms. It does not, in other words, have a beginning, a middle, and an end, nor any of the conventions which we normally associate with narrative. What remains constant in Trakl's poetry is not a single line of events that governs the meaning of individual poems, but rather certain sets of images which keep reappearing throughout his work in varying relationships with one another. Instead of "using" the individual poems to extrapolate some such larger narrative which seems implied in the background, the critic is, I think, on firmer ground if he starts by asking himself to precisely what effect Trakl is combining his characteristic images in a particular poem.

As indicated in the last chapter, Trakl's imagery can be divided roughly into two areas: benign, pastoral images, on the one hand, and malign, often demonic images, on the other. The most common type of benign imagery is the nocturnal landscape illustrated in "An den Knaben Elis," though it can also take the form of the South Sea paradise of "Psalm" or the traditional, ordered life of the countryman in "Helian" who "carries bread and wine in clean hands" (l. 18). Benign imagery is associated sometimes with a past world of innocence, as in the "Elis" poems, and sometimes with the process of expiation. Malign images intrude in varying ways from poem to poem, and, by the same token, the relationship between the

two groups of images shifts from poem to poem. Sometimes the
malign images destroy a landscape of innocence while at other
times benign images work to overcome a demonic landscape.
Sometimes the balance remains precarious throughout a poem.
Benign images at times carry unpleasant overtones, while some
malign images have an unexpectedly pleasing aspect to them.
Instead of a single, all-pervasive narrative that "stands behind"
all the poems, there are, in effect, as many "narratives" in Trakl
as there are poems—or, for that matter, as there are drafts of
poems. The individual poem—even the earliest sketch for a
poem—is a means by which Trakl can effect a fresh interaction
among his various strains of images. Each poem becomes a new
means of coping with reality. From one poem to the next, the
basic components are essentially the same, but their arrange-
ment and the feelings with which they are presented change.
They are like counters in a game, shifting their values according to their position on the board.

"An den Knaben Elis" dramatizes the poet's attempt to
invoke a world of lost innocence which he can never quite
capture in its purity. Images of suffering or negation—the
bramble bush, the recognition of Elis' pastness, the black cave,
and the animal lowering its lids—intrude with increasing intensity. Trakl's direct address to Elis throughout the poem is a
rhetorical sign of his struggle to recapture the world which
Elis represents. Through the regularity of the tercets, which
correspond to the syntactical units throughout most of the poem,
Trakl is able to suggest the harmony of Elis' world; through the
run-on between the fifth and sixth stanzas, he suggests, in turn,
the difficulty of sustaining his vision of this world. The reader's
most vivid apprehension of Elis comes at the poem's center, in
the image of the boy moving his arms "in the blue." Rhetor-
ically, this is a poem of praise, like a psalm or a love lyric: Elis
comes to life for us through the poet's act of praise for him.
Gradually, throughout the first half of the poem, Elis and his
world are brought into focus, but in the last half the focus
breaks down. In the first half Elis is an active being, "walking
into the night" and "moving his arms." In the last half he has
become passive, and we glimpse him only through the parts
of his body—moonlike eyes, temples, trunk ("Leib" can mean
either "body" or "trunk"). By the end of the poem, Elis seems
vastly distant, yet something of his past loveliness remains. The

final line creates the kind of ambivalent resolution which is frequent in Trakl's poetry: the word "gold" is qualified by "final," "stars" by "ruined," with each of these holding the other in balance.

If "An den Knaben Elis" eulogizes Elis to evoke a world of innocence, the other "Elis" poem, entitled simply "Elis," describes the total breakdown of this world and ends on a note of total desolation. Trakl uses sets of images similar to those found in "An den Knaben Elis," yet manipulates them in distinctly different ways:

1

Vollkommen ist die Stille dieses goldenen Tags.
Unter alten Eichen
Erscheinst du, Elis, ein Ruhender mit runden Augen.

Ihre Bläue spiegelt den Schlummer der Liebenden.
An deinem Mund
Verstummten ihre rosigen Seufzer.

Am Abend zog der Fischer die schweren Netze ein.
Ein guter Hirt
Führt seine Herde am Waldsaum hin.
O! wie gerecht sind, Elis, alle deine Tage.

Leise sinkt
An kahlen Mauern des Ölbaums blaue Stille,
Erstirbt eines Greisen dunkler Gesang.

Ein goldener Kahn
Schaukelt, Elis, dein Herz am einsamen Himmel.

2

Ein sanftes Glockenspiel tönt in Elis' Brust
Am Abend,
Da sein Haupt ins schwarze Kissen sinkt.

   Ein blaues Wild
Blutet leise im Dornengestrüpp.

Ein brauner Baum steht abgeschieden da;
Seine blauen Früchte fielen von ihm.

Zeichen und Sterne
Versinken leise im Abendweiher.

Hinter dem Hügel ist es Winter geworden.

Blaue Tauben
Trinken nachts den eisigen Schweiss,
Der von Elis' kristallener Stirne rinnt.

Immer tönt
An schwarzen Mauern Gottes einsamer Wind.

1

1   Perfect [complete] is the stillness of this golden day.
2   Under aged oaks
3   You, Elis, appear a reposing one [in repose] with
        round eyes.

4   Their blueness mirrors the slumber of the lovers.
5   On your mouth
6   Their rosy sighs fell silent.

7   In the evening the fisherman drew in his heavy nets.
8   A good shepherd
9   Leads his herd along the forest's edge.
10 Oh how just are, Elis, all your days.

11 Softly
12 The olive tree's blue stillness sinks along bare walls,
13 The dark song of an old man dies away.

14 A golden boat,
15 Your heart, Elis, rocks in the lonely sky.

2

16 A soft chiming of bells sounds in Elis' breast
17 In the evening,
18 When his head sinks into the black cushion.

19   A blue animal [deer]
20 Bleeds softly in the bramble bushes.

21 A brown tree stands there dead [secluded];
22 Its blue fruits fell down from it.

23   Signs and stars
24   Sink down [disappear] softly in the evening-pond.

25   Behind the hill it has become winter.

26   Blue doves
27   At night drink the icy sweat
28   That runs down from Elis' crystal forehead.

29   Constantly [always]
30   Along black walls God's lonely wind sounds.

(I, 85-86)

Like "An den Knaben Elis," this poem starts out as an
attempt to recapture Elis and his world through praise. Indeed, as
the critical edition shows, the two poems were evidently conceived as a single poem, with "An den Knaben Elis" as a kind
of prelude to "Elis."[5] But in the course of composition Trakl
must have realized that each poem was taking its own direction.
Only at moments does "Elis" strike the same note as "An den
Knaben Elis," for instance in the line "Oh how just are, Elis, all
your days," which, like the similarly shaped line, "Oh how long,
Elis, you have been dead," voices the speaker's desperate longing
for Elis' lost world. Except for this line, however, Trakl maintains a far cooler, more distant tone in "Elis" than in the other
poem. For "Elis" is a poem of vaster scope, one which, within
its thirty lines, attempts to map out the process by which an
idyllic world gradually breaks down into its antithesis. As in
"Helian," Trakl's Symbolist method allows him to achieve a
maximum range of reference with a minimum amount of
explicatory statement. And, again as in "Helian," Trakl draws
some of his most memorable images from other literary sources
that must have been floating through his mind at the time.
"Elis" could, in fact, be described as a pastiche. The lines about
the fisherman and the shepherd (11. 7-9) allude to two passages
in the Gospel of John (21:11 and 10:11-13, respectively). The
moon as a golden boat in the sky (11. 14-15) unmistakably echoes
a passage from Nietzsche's *Also sprach Zarathustra*. The image
of Elis sinking his head into the pillow (1. 18) may have been
suggested by Hoffmann's version of the Elis Fröbom story, and
the reference to the old man's song (1. 13) by Hofmannsthal's
version. Finally, the images of icy sweat (11. 27-28) and God's
wind (1. 30) echo Ammer's Rimbaud.[6] A source study on the

scale of Livingston Lowes's *Road to Xanadu* could probably
trace a model for every line; for both Coleridge and Trakl, the
use of narcotics may well have caused images from widely
varying contexts to be held in suspension at the same time.

But the most pervasive influence on the poem was the famous
lyric by Hölderlin, "Hälfte des Lebens" ("Middle of Life"),
written about 1803, which not only suggested the images of the
walls and winter but also created the mythological framework
which informs the poem as a whole. Like "Elis," Hölderlin's lyric,
which in its lack of rhetorical connectives anticipates Symbolist
poetry, contrasts two opposed visions of life:

> Mit gelben Birnen hänget
> Und voll mit wilden Rosen
> Das Land in den See,
> Ihr holden Schwäne,
> Und trunken von Küssen
> Tunkt ihr das Haupt
> Ins heilignüchterne Wasser.

> Weh mir, wo nehm' ich, wenn
> Es Winter ist, die Blumen, und wo
> Den Sonnenschein,
> Und Schatten der Erde?
> Die Mauern stehn
> Sprachlos und kalt, im Winde
> Klirren die Fahnen.

> With yellow pears
> And full of wild roses
> The land hangs down into the lake,
> You gracious [lovely] swans,
> And drunk with kisses
> You dip your heads
> Into the holy-sober water.

> Alas, [from] where shall I take
> The flowers, when it is winter, and where
> The sunshine,
> And shadow of the earth?
> The walls stand
> Speechless and cold, in the wind
> The weather vanes clatter.[7]

Hölderlin's two stanzas correspond to the beginning and the end, respectively, of Trakl's poem. Compared to "Elis," Hölderlin's poem is notable, in fact, for the conciseness and absoluteness with which these two aspects (or "halves") of life are separated from one another. The first stanza, with its heavy-hanging pears (like the similarly ripe grapes in "An den Knaben Elis") and its lovely swans, suddenly gives way to a world of total bleakness, without flowers, warmth, or even shadows to remind him of an earth that was once benign.

Hölderlin achieves his sharpness of contrast largely through the power of the images themselves—at one extreme, yellow pears hanging *into* the lake (the German accusative renders the meeting of pears and lake with an immediacy impossible in English), at the other extreme, the weather vanes clattering desolately in the cold wind. The contrast is defined by the syntactical movement as well: note, for instance, the difference between the powerfully flowing sentence of the first stanza and the broken phrases ("wo nehm ich, wenn/Es Winter ist, die Blumen . . .") of the second, or the difference between the direct address of the poet to the swans in the first stanza (the use of the second person asserts his intimacy with the scene) and the self-questioning of the isolated poet in the second stanza. Syntactically the poem moves, one might say, from enthusiastic invocation to a rhetorical question which can only meet with the reply "nowhere."

The absoluteness of Hölderlin's contrast gives this poem an overwhelmingly tragic force. Trakl obviously does not strive for so sharply tragic an effect: "Elis," in fact, like most of his poems, is notable for the tentativeness with which he mediates between his contrasting visions. The poem consists essentially of a succession of images gradually shifting from a paradise-like scene, a moment of perfection and fulfillment (the poem's first word, "Vollkommen," encompasses both these meanings), to a barren, fallen world. As always in Trakl's free verse, one notes the constantly shifting perspectives, the exclamatory intrusions, and the sudden changes of tense. And yet one can discern here a very definite line of progression from each stanza to the next. The third stanza, for instance, though it presents two relatively benign pastoral images, shows traces of underlying fear: the fisherman draws his nets in to protect them from the uncertainties of night, while the good shepherd skirts the forest's edge, as though at the border of the unknown.

The subtle transitions throughout the poem are suggested not only by the image content of the individual stanzas but also through various rhetorical signals. One could, in fact, speak of a "vocabulary of transition" that Trakl employs not only in this poem but throughout his mature work. For instance, the verbs "fallen" and "sinken" ("to fall" and "to sink")—used to portray the transition from one state to another at several points in "Elis" (11. 11, 18, 22, 24)—recur in a large proportion of other poems as well; indeed, a word count of Trakl's mature work has shown "sinken" to be his most frequently used verb.[8] In "Elis" and elsewhere, one can find such prefixes as *ver* and *er*, which in German add a sense of process to a verb (for example, "erstirbt" ["dies away"] in 1. 13). Transitions generally occur very slowly in Trakl, as is evident in his constant reiteration of words suggesting quietness and gentleness: in "Elis" the word "leise" ("soft," "gentle," "quiet") is used three times; "Stille" ("stillness"), twice; and "sanft" ("soft," "gentle"), once. "Leise" and "sanft," I might add, are two of Trakl's five most frequently used adjectives.[9]

Besides these words of transition, other devices such as tense shift and word placement record the changes taking place from moment to moment in the poem. In the third stanza, for example, the harmoniousness suggested by the images of the fisherman and the shepherd is amplified through the peculiar balance achieved by the line "Oh how just are, Elis, all your days" (one need only shift the name Elis as follows—"Oh Elis, how just are all your days"—to destroy the balance, not only of the line, but of the entire stanza). Moreover, the sudden shift from present to past tense in line 22 serves to underline the increasing distance from the moment of perfection at the opening of the poem. Even the placement of images within a single line defines a stage in the transition process. Take, for example, the line "An kahlen Mauern des Ölbaums blaue Stille" ("Along bare walls the olive tree's blue stillness"). Here, as Trakl approaches the "midway" point between the contrasting visions which open and close the poem, the relatively positive image of "blue stillness" is set against the negatively directed "bare walls," while between them stands the two-edged image of the olive tree, with its traditional connotations of peacefulness, as well as its implicit association with the sufferings of Christ. The midway point itself is marked by the sharpest single break within the process of transition: as he begins Section II, he shifts abruptly from the second to the third person, from direct invocation of the gradually more distant Elis to a description of him in narrative terms.

The mythological framework which "Elis" derives from "Hälfte des Lebens" is indicative of certain processes of thought which Trakl's later poetry owes to Hölderlin's work as a whole.[10] Hölderlin's mythology, like that of Blake and Yeats, encompasses at once a view of public history and of the progress of the individual mind. His conception of history includes, for example, a vision of ancient Greece as a state of harmony when, at certain privileged moments at least, men could stand in intimate, unselfconscious relationship to their gods. For Hölderlin the last of these gods was Christ, whose death was followed by a long dark age, which, in turn, was to be succeeded, through the mediation of poets, by a restoration of something of the original harmony which once existed between the divine and human orders. Hölderlin's dialectic of history is paralleled by a view of the growth and development of the individual, who moves from an early state of unity through a "fall" into a state of self-consciousness, and thence progresses toward a restoration, on a new and higher level, of the lost powers of the past. I have obviously oversimplified Hölderlin's complex dialectic, yet have tried at least to indicate something of the solid framework of thought that stands behind his individual poems. "Hälfte des Lebens" obviously focuses on private rather than public history; the early drafts of its two stanzas, moreover, were not originally designed for the same poem but happened to be among jottings on the same sheet of paper.[11] The apparently accidental nature of its conception is hardly typical of Hölderlin and is, in fact, closer in spirit to Trakl's own method of composition.

Serious criticism of Hölderlin must proceed, in one way or another, from a knowledge of the mythological and dialectical framework out of which his poems are built. Just as every critic of Blake nowadays has to take cognizance of the work of Northrop Frye, who provided the first adequate description of the structure of Blake's mythology, so every Hölderlin critic must at least start from those accounts of the Hölderlinian dialectic which Friedrich Beissner and his students have been able to work out.[12]

One would feel comfortable to know that Trakl's mythological framework can be uncovered and that the reader could learn to interpret his individual poems in terms of a similar framework. But the general coherence that one could attribute to the private mythologies of poets such as Hölderlin and Blake is, as far as I can tell, absent in Trakl. As I have indicated earlier in this chapter, instead of a larger mythology which we can use as a key to individual poems, we have only the *semblance* of a mythology. Earlier I noted the various components of a mythology which run persistently through Trakl's poetry—the contrasting positive and negative visions, the protagonist as murderer and penitent, and the sister as victim and beatific vision.

Beginning in early 1913, but to some extent already in "Psalm" and "Helian," Trakl comes increasingly to order these so-called components into historical sequences. Images which, in his earlier poems, appear to coexist in time now begin to assume temporal relationships to one another. Thus, throughout his later poetry we gain the illusion of vast transformations, of benign forces in the process of disintegration, of demonic forces, in turn, supplanted by benign ones, of sudden intrusions of the past and equally sudden projections into an unexpected future, of one vision of life vainly trying to stabilize itself against the pressures of another. In Trakl, even more than in Hölderlin, we become aware of the processes and transitions by which one state gives way to its opposite; his world, as a result, is full of purgatorial journeys, descents into hell, seasonal changes, wanderers entering new phases of experience.

If Rimbaud suggested the disjunctions of language by which Trakl might express his peculiar vision, Hölderlin, one might say, suggested the structures of thought within which this vision could be embodied.[13] We can think of Trakl, as we do of Hölderlin or Blake, as what critics nowadays call a "mythopoeic" poet, that is, one who speaks not so much a discursive language as a language of images; whose images, moreover, retain a definable, though often loose, relationship to one another from one poem to the next; and who attempts to renew some of the meanings latent within comparable images in earlier poets. While the blue nocturnal imagery of the "Elis" poems, in one sense, remains a kind of constant throughout Trakl's later work, its functions change subtly to meet the needs of individual poems. Thus, whereas in "An den Knaben Elis" Trakl uses blueness to evoke

Elis' world in all its immediacy ("Your lips drink the coolness of the blue rock-spring"), in "Elis" he introduces this imagery for instance, in the blue fruits which have already fallen from the dead tree—only to stress its evanescent quality. As a type of pastoral, moreover, this imagery is both distinct in itself (indeed, the blue world is virtually Trakl's trademark) and a renewal of a traditional pastoral archetype.

One could argue that Trakl's use of images enables him to express emotion more precisely and, in fact, more comfortably than would be possible in a less metaphoric form of statement. "An den Knaben Elis" portrays intense longing with a fervor that Trakl might not have found possible if he had addressed a being more easily identifiable than the boy Elis. The sense of quiet, elegiac regret which pervades the poem "Elis" results, to a great degree, from the stylized precision with which the moment of perfection at the opening is made to recede from us in both time and space.

By constructing his poetic world out of images which have a mythical aura about them, Trakl also succeeds in endowing each poem with a greater range of reference than he could by means of more discursive expression. On its most literal level, "Elis" is a poem about the gradual extinction of Elis' world. But a statement of this kind does not even begin to exhaust the poem's range of meaning, for the poem deals at once with the process of physical death, the death of poetic inspiration, cosmic disintegration, the change of seasons from summer to winter, and the declining condition of man in human history. The complex effect of such poems is dependent upon what might seem a contradictory set of intentions: Trakl's image patterns seek to define emotions precisely, yet at the same time they open up into a remarkably wide range of meanings within the context of the individual poem.

II *Three Lyrics of Process: "Am Mönchsberg,"*
"Sonja," and "Ein Winterabend"

A large proportion of Trakl's shorter lyrics can be read as "moments" in the transitional process between the positive and negative extremes of Trakl's world. In the remainder of this chapter I shall look at three short lyrics, all dating from the last half of 1913: "Am Mönchsberg," which is typical of many that portray this process through images of wandering; "Sonja," which, by "borrowing" a character from Dostoevsky, transfers this process to an explicitly moral world of guilt and penitence; and "Ein Winterabend," which, by presenting the possibility of a "happy" outcome to the journey, works in a direction precisely opposite to that of "Elis." I start with "Am Mönchsberg":

> Wo im Schatten herbstlicher Ulmen der verfallene Pfad
>   hinabsinkt,
> Ferne den Hütten von Laub, schlafenden Hirten,
> Immer folgt dem Wandrer die dunkle Gestalt der Kühle
>
> Über knöchernen Steg, die hyazinthene Stimme des Knaben,
> Leise sagend die vergessene Legende des Walds,
> Sanfter ein Krankes nun die wilde Klage des Bruders.
>
> Also rührt ein spärliches Grün das Knie des Fremdlings,
> Das versteinerte Haupt;
> Näher rauscht der blaue Quell die Klage der Frauen.

1 Where in the shadow of autumnal elms the ruined
   [fallen] path sinks downward,
2 Far from the huts of foliage [tabernacles], from
   sleeping shepherds,
3 Always [still] the dark shape of coolness follows the
   wanderer

4 Over [the] bony footpath, the hyacinthian voice of
   the boy,
5 Quietly telling the forgotten legend of the forest,
6 More softly a sick thing now the wild lament of the
   brother.

7 Thus scanty green [greenery] touches the knee of the
   stranger,
8 The petrified head;
9 More closely the blue spring murmurs the lament of
   the women.

(I, 94)

"Am Mönchsberg" enacts a drama of transformations in about as compressed a form as can be found in Trakl's work. The rhetoric is purely descriptive; even the exclamatory intrusions and second-person invocations of the "Elis" poems are missing. The poem opens *in medias res*; the opening word, "Where," which is used as a subordinating conjunction, gives the illusion, from the start, of a past narrative of which this poem presumably narrates only a small portion. Past participles ("ruined path," "forgotten legend") indicate a past with both idyllic and negative overtones. The faraway tabernacles and sleeping shepherds are mentioned to remind us of idyllic moments that are removed from the scene in space as well as in time. As usual in Trakl, the action of the poem involves a downward movement, a sinking or falling: it is where the ruined path sinks downward that the transformations are about to take place.

The setting is both actual and symbolic. The Mönchsberg is a forested hill that juts into Salzburg; yet the name means literally Monk's Hill, with obvious overtones suggesting a withdrawal from the world. Even if one ignores its relationship to that of Trakl's other poems, the imagery suggests a sense of renewal, the shedding of a wild and burdensome past. The "dark shape of coolness," "the murmuring blue spring," the "scanty green" that touches the stranger—all contain an intrinsically refreshing quality. The "bony footpath" and "petrified head" suggest something hard, even brittle, as though objects must harden and break before they can be renewed. The dimness of the setting, which rejects the absolutes of light and dark, indicates a world which is at once mysterious and in a state of transition and which, potentially, could move in the direction of either extreme.

A complex combination of verbal resources works to define the transformations within the poem. Comparative forms such as "more softly" and "more closely" indicate a sense of process. Adverbs of time such as "always" and "now" and the present participle "telling" are signals, as it were, of the immediacy of the process. The word order works powerfully throughout the poem to create the illusion that disparate objects are closely linked to one another: in lines 3, 7, and 9 of the German text the subjects and objects of the verbs are set directly next to each other, while the verbs that link these subjects and objects are placed before the nouns. This illusion is also achieved through Trakl's piling up of nouns and phrases in apposition to one another: "tabernacles" with "sleeping shepherds," "dark shape" with "hyacinthian voice," "knee of a stranger" with "petrified head."

Trakl's manipulation of syntax in this poem creates an effect of stylization far greater than that found in any of the earlier poems I have discussed. After mid-1913, in fact, all of Trakl's poetry is characterized by an increasingly stylized language.

In "Am Mönchsberg," written in September, 1913, the subduing
of the women's lament by the blue spring in the final stanza
involves a poetic distortion of language through the use of
"murmurs" as a transitive verb. Even more daring is the untranslatable construction "ein Krankes" (l. 6), in which the
adjective "krank" ("sick") is made into a neuter noun and preceded by the indefinite article. This construction, which was
undoubtedly suggested to Trakl by several examples in the later
Hölderlin,[14] was to become more and more frequent in his own
later work. It serves two functions: first, it adds to the stylized
effect of the poem and thus helps suggest an autonomous world
removed from everyday reality; secondly, it provides a way for
Trakl to allude to the quality of a thing without committing
himself to any recognizable objects in a real world. To put it
differently, Trakl wants to talk about sickness as a substantial
being: he therefore needs a noun to achieve the sense of substance; but a conventional abstract noun such as "Krankheit"
("sickness") has too little substance, while the masculine or
feminine noun—"ein Kranker" or "eine Kranke" ("a sick man"
or "a sick woman")—commits him to a specific person and takes
the emphasis away from the quality of sickness. German gram-
mar, theoretically at least, permits a construction such as "ein
Krankes," though the term would have no meaning outside the
context of the poem.

Trakl's refusal to commit himself to real and recognizable
objects is evident also in the way he has fragmented the protagonist of the poem. The wanderer, the brother, the stranger,
perhaps also the boy (his hyacinthian voice relates him to Elis)
are at once aspects of the same being; but Trakl is more interested
in the various aspects than in the concrete being that may or
may not stand behind them. The poem refuses to be about any
particular protagonist but is centered, rather, around the processes of transformation taking place within some being or beings.

Except for the word "thus," which introduces the last stanza,
Trakl gives little indication that these processes of transformation
are resolved with any finality. "Positive" and "negative" elements,
in fact, remain in a kind of unresolved balance, with the "scanty
green" qualifying "petrified head," and "blue spring" working
to transform "lament of the women." An earlier version of the
poem ends on a much more "positive" note:

Weich umschmeichelt ein spärliches Grün das Knie des
    Fremdlings,
Ein milder Gott die sehr ermüdete Stirn,
Tastet silbern der Schritt in die Stille zurück.

Softly a scanty green caresses the knee of the stranger,
A gentle God [caresses] the very fatigued forehead;
The step [stride] gropes its way silverly back into the
    stillness.

(I, 381)

The conciliatory ending of this early version works to undermine
both the irresolution and the sense of activity which dominate
the final version from beginning to end. The introduction of
the mild God who caresses, moreover, adds a sentimental note
which Trakl nearly always suppressed before completing a poem.

If the final version of "Am Mönchsberg" dramatizes process
in a peculiarly active way, "Sonja" approaches process in an
equally passive way:

Abend kehrt in alten Garten;
Sonjas Leben, blaue Stille.
Wilder Vögel Wanderfahrten;
Kahler Baum in Herbst und Stille.

Sonnenblume, sanftgeneigte
Über Sonjas weisses Leben.
Wunde, rote, niegezeigte
Lässt in dunklen Zimmern leben,

Wo die blauen Glocken läuten;
Sonjas Schritt und sanfte Stille.
Sterbend Tier grüsst im Entgleiten,
Kahler Baum in Herbst und Stille.

Sonne alter Tage leuchtet
Über Sonjas weisse Brauen,
Schnee, der ihre Wangen feuchtet,
Und die Wildnis ihrer Brauen.

1	Evening returns into [the] old garden;	a
2	Sonia's life, blue stillness.	b
3	Wild birds' migrations;	a
4	Bare tree in fall and stillness.	b

5   Sunflower, softly bent
6   Over Sonia's white life.
7   Wound, red, never shown
8   Causes [Sonia] to live in dark rooms,

9   Where the blue bells ring;
10 Sonia's step and soft stillness.
11 Dying animal greets while slipping away,
12 Bare tree in fall and stillness.

13 Sun of ancient days shines
14 Over Sonia's white brows,
15 Snow, which moistens her cheeks,
16 And the wilderness of her brows.

(I, 105)

The title character of this poem is undergoing a kind of transition, yet the changes that take place within her are defined not by means of wanderings, as in "Am Mönchsberg" and innumerable other Trakl poems, but through the imagery surrounding her. One could best describe the poem as a portrait, and, as such, it maintains an essentially static outward quality. This static quality is confirmed, as it were, by the rhyming of identical words in the second and fourth lines of each stanza. Moreover, if "Am Mönchsberg" was notable for the transitive power of its verbs, "Sonja" is notable for a corresponding "intransitiveness." Thus, such verbs as "lassen" ("allow," "cause"—1. 8) and "grüssen" ("greet"—1. 11), which normally take direct objects, are conspicuous here for the difficulty they cause the reader in determining what their objects are. The poem is dominated by its nouns, most of which are not connected with verbs. One notes, in addition, the absence of articles before many nouns, a phenomenon frequent in the German folk-song tradition: "bare tree" instead of "the bare tree," "sunflower," "wound," "dying animal," "sun," "snow." As a result, the effect which Trakl achieves is one of great immediacy, as though there were no barriers between the poet and the objects he is trying to evoke.

Although most Trakl poems are portrayals of actions, with verbs in a dominant position, this is a poem directed at objects, with the actions merely implied. We are shown very little of Sonia directly, for Trakl, characteristically interweaving elements of the human and natural world, concentrates on the penitential atmosphere surrounding her—the dark room, the bare tree, the stillness he so repeatedly invokes. External objects, one might say, become tokens of internal processes which the poem never explicitly describes.

Yet Trakl finds indirect ways of probing the subject of his portrait, as in the extraordinary succession of words which make up line 7: "Wound, red, never shown," which proceeds from noun to modifying adjective and finally to a modifying past participle. The line creates the effect of a gradual and painful uncovering of the wound itself; one need merely try it out in regular word order—"red wound that has never been shown"—to note its power. Yet Trakl also has the decorum to withdraw from this exploration of Sonia's mind, for his focus in the succeeding line moves quickly back to the objects surrounding her. The poem is in four-foot trochees, the traditional meter of the German folk song, a form which, through the expectations it evokes in the reader, does not lend itself easily to psychological probing, except in the most implicit and delicate manner. Thus, the seventh line is one of those unexpected intrusions that momentarily threaten to break the framework of a poem; the line, as a result, has the effect of a great illumination; it is a type of effect, moreover, that Trakl could not have achieved in free verse, which by its nature lacks the strict framework against which an intrusion of this sort can take place.

"Sonja" is significant not simply as an illustration of Trakl's private imagery accommodating itself to a traditional form of lyric but also as an example of Trakl's imagery interacting with the world of another author. Strictly speaking, "Sonja" was not directly written about the heroine of *Crime and Punishment* but about a young girl whom Trakl knew and to whom he gave the name of Dostoevsky's heroine.[15] In a more fundamental sense, however, Dostoevsky's vision of life dominates this poem. Rimbaud, as we have seen, provided Trakl with the essential language for his mature poetry, and Hölderlin, the semblance of a mythical framework; Dostoevsky, by contrast, contributed the moral framework for Trakl's poetic world. From Dostoevsky, for instance, come the often frantic alternations between fall and grace, together with the transformations taking place within Trakl's protagonists, who sometimes alternate between the roles of murderer and monk within the confines of a single poem. The figure of Sonia, whatever actual girl Trakl had in mind when he wrote the poem, is an extension of the sister-figure found throughout his poetry. Just as Trakl's male protagonists run the widest possible moral gamut, so his female figures (often they are referred to explicitly as the "sister") move between the role of whore or murderess and that of a celestial being who appears at the end of many poems as a vision of beatitude.

In this poem Sonia stands at a midpoint between these extremes. The past which Trakl projects here takes two forms—the red wound, a token of her sin, and the "sun of ancient days," which, with the sunflower and the old garden, suggest the processes by which Sonia's wound may be healed. The gesture of "greeting" by the dying animal that is "slipping away" is, like the wound itself, one of those sudden illuminations which serve to define Sonia's predicament for us: the animal is an analogue, a fellow sufferer, who, like Sonia, is in the process of transformation. The bare tree, the stillness, and the autumnal atmosphere provide the natural setting for transformations, and the two extremes between which Sonia stands are held in balance throughout the poem.

But the word "wilderness" in the last line, which echoes the wildness of the birds in the opening stanza, puts the final stress on Sonia's past and her destructive potentialities. The word seems all the more startling because it is set against images of snow and whiteness, which here and in many other Trakl poems are figures for the leprous scabs which fall from the face during the process of penitence. It is remarkable, one might add, how much of the poem speaks for itself without recourse to these poems. As long as the reader is aware of the Dostoevsky allusion, which establishes penitence as the poem's theme, all the images except perhaps the snow and the blueness "make sense" without a knowledge of Trakl's work as a whole. At the same time every image remains fully characteristic of his work.

In much the same way, "Ein Winterabend," another of Trakl's few rhymed poems written in late 1913, reveals itself without mediation to the uninitiated; yet it was precisely this poem that was chosen by one critic, T. J. Casey, as a kind of paradigm to explicate the range of meanings within Trakl's vocabulary as a whole.[16] Though "Sonja" ended somewhat ambiguously, with both the positive and negative extremes of Trakl's world set precariously in balance, "Ein Winterabend" must be seen as a poem moving toward an uncomplicatedly benign vision:

Wenn der Schnee ans Fenster fällt,
Lang die Abendglocke läutet,
Vielen ist der Tisch bereitet
Und das Haus ist wohlbestellt.

Mancher auf der Wanderschaft
Kommt ans Tor auf dunklen Pfaden.
Golden blüht der Baum der Gnaden
Aus der Erde kühlem Saft.

Wanderer tritt still herein;
Schmerz versteinerte die Schwelle.
Da erglänzt in reiner Helle
Auf dem Tische Brot und Wein.

1	When the snow falls against the window,	a
2	The evening bell rings long,	b
3	The table is prepared for many,	b
4	And the house is well appointed.	a

5	Many a one on his travels
6	Approaches the gate on dark paths.
7	Golden blooms the tree of grace
8	From the earth's cool sap.

9	Wanderer quietly steps inside;
10	Pain has petrified the threshold.
11	Then shines forth in pure brightness
12	On the table bread and wine.

(I, 102)

I have deliberately strained English syntax in the last two lines of my translation in order to render the climactic order of the words: first, the notion of something shining forth; next the pure brightness, which suggests a celestial dimension within the poem's largely domestic setting; then the table, which returns the reader momentarily to concrete domestic reality (though by its context it also evokes the table of the Last Supper); and finally the bread and wine, which, through their traditional Christian meaning, fuse the earthly and spiritual into a single powerful image.

The poem is organized, throughout, to culminate in this final image. The first stanza sets the scene—the sheltered, well-appointed household with the winter storm raging outside. The stress remains on the domesticity of the setting: only by the end of the poem do we become aware of the spiritual meanings implicit in the evening bell or the table.

Since the table implies a guest, the scene of the first stanza in effect prepares us for the traveler who appears in the second stanza. The scene shifts back momentarily to the outside, and we glance at the wanderer approaching on dark paths, which contrasts significantly with the light and ordered world within. The gnomic last two lines of this stanza, by reference to the cross and the revitalizing powers of the earth, are the first indications of a larger context within which the poem's images must be seen.

Just as the first stanza, with its inviting table, implies the second, so the second, through its image of the wanderer approaching the door, implies the third stanza. With the wanderer's entrance into the house, the inside and the outside worlds are finally brought together. The stanza's second line, with its reference to pain, serves as a reminder of the sufferings that one might associate with the dark paths on which the guest had wandered. Significantly, the sufferings are mentioned in the past tense, "petrified," as it were, in the threshold which protects inside from outside. This allusion to past sufferings is only momentary, yet its presence in the poem enhances the effect of the benign vision toward which Trakl moves in the last two lines.

The effect of the poem is precisely the opposite of that conveyed by "Elis"; whereas the latter poem moves toward a vision of death, "Ein Winterabend" moves toward the assertion of a human order in which divine grace directly intervenes. Yet in an earlier version of this poem which Trakl sent in a letter to Karl Kraus, the resolution was as ambiguous as that of "Sonja." In this early version, whose first six lines remain unchanged in the printed text, the last half reads as follows:

> Seine Wunde voller Gnaden
> Pflegt der Liebe sanfte Kraft.
>
> O! des Menschen blosse Pein.
> Der mit Engeln stumm gerungen,
> Langt von heiligem Schmerz bezwungen
> Still nach Gottes Brot und Wein.
>
> His wound full of grace
> Is nursed by love's gentle power.

> Oh! Man's naked agony.
> He who struggled silently with angels,
> Overcome by holy pain, reaches out
> Quietly for God's bread and wine.
>   (I, 383)

Like the conclusion of numerous other Trakl poems, the resolution here is suspended somewhere between the extremes of agony and grace. The bread and wine (here explicitly associated with God, as though Trakl needed to spell out the spiritual meanings of the symbols to offset the strong emphasis on suffering) are merely "reached for" without the certainty of grace symbolized by the "pure brightness" in the final version. Indeed, in this early draft, Trakl had not yet achieved that delicate balance between spiritual and domestic, inside order and outside suffering, which characterizes the completed poem.

Just as "Elis" reworks and reinterprets the theme and structure of Hölderlin's "Hälfte des Lebens," "Ein Winterabend" assimilates the conventions of the German folk song to Trakl's poetic world. Except for the ninth line, in which the verb "petrified" is an easily identifiable Trakl mannerism, the poem could almost pass for a folk song, or at least as a typical Romantic imitation of that form. The imagery is characteristically Trakl's, but in meter, tone, and syntax the poem approaches the manner of writers such as Eichendorff and Uhland. As in numerous Romantic (and folk) poems, "Ein Winterabend" maintains an antithesis between the secure, well-ordered world of the household and the uncertainties of wandering within the outside world. The syntax is simple throughout, though with a deliberately archaic flavor to simulate the language of folk song. By thus submitting himself to the conventions of an older form, Trakl demonstrates a flexibility far greater than one would think attainable within the confines of his private imagery and Symbolist technique.

CHAPTER 5

Toward the Demonic Image: Poems of 1914

I "Traum und Umnachtung"

ALTHOUGH "Sonja," "Ein Winterabend," and a few other rhymed poems of late 1913 achieve a simplicity rare in Trakl's mature work, the poems written during his last months are notable for their high degree of complexity and their increased use of personal mannerisms. One of the most difficult (and also most beautiful) of these poems, "Frühling der Seele" ("Spring-time of the Soul" [I, 141-42]), written early in 1914, was, in fact, utilized by an antimodernist critic to attack Trakl's work in general for what he condemns as obscurity and the failure to engage adequately with the real world.[1] Trakl's imagery in this poem is not essentially different from that of the "Elis" poems or "Am Mönchsberg," but the organization and the verbal texture are more complex. The reader who rejects the "Elis" poems will of course reject the later poems as well; yet these later poems are accessible, I think, by essentially the same mode of reading which I have tried to demonstrate for the earlier ones.

The poems in this chapter all represent significant aspects of the final phase of Trakl's poetry. The prose poem "Traum und Umnachtung" ("Dream and Madness"), written in January, 1914, fuses the methods of prose narrative with Trakl's poetic tech-niques to create a personal drama of visionary proportions; "Das Gewitter" ("The Thunderstorm"), one of seven related poems—all completed between May and July, 1914—is written in terse, exclamatory lines and attempts a new, more assertive mode of expression; and his last poems, "Grodek" and "Klage" ("Lament"), written on the eastern front in September, 1914, use Trakl's characteristic private images to come to terms with the actual cataclysm which had been hovering in his imagination all along. Above all, as I shall stress in this chapter, many of Trakl's late poems contain an intense, peculiarly demonic quality that manifests itself in various new forms of language in which he was experimenting during his last year.

"Traum und Umnachtung" is by far the longest of Trakl's four prose poems and thus the longest single work among his mature writings. It follows two prose poems from late 1913, "Verwandlung des Bösen" ("Transformation of Evil" [I, 97-98]) and "Winternacht" ("Winter Night" [I, 128]), both of them as identifiably Trakl's as any of his poems in verse, yet also more anecdotal in nature. Neither of these works, however, seems to me of the same stature as "Traum und Umnachtung," which, together with the last prose poem, "Offenbarung und Untergang" ("Revelation and Fall" [I, 168-70]), composed in May, 1914, stands as one of Trakl's major achievements, comparable in quality to the best of his lyrics, yet greater in scope and intensity than all except "Helian."

A number of prose poems, or prose sketches of a highly lyrical type, can be found among Trakl's juvenilia (I, 189-201). But none of these is in any significant way related to the four later prose poems. Rather, these later works are a direct outgrowth of the scenes, images, and verbal peculiarities of his free verse. One critic has actually tried to set the four poems into verse lines;[2] and although these lines are, superficially at least, indistinguishable from Trakl's free verse, the peculiar effects which Trakl achieves in these poems result directly from their prose form. Printed as prose, the poems attain a rapidity of movement and an illusion of narrative fullness absent from the poems written in free verse. Take, for instance, these lines from "Helian":

A pale angel,
The son steps into the empty house of his fathers.

The sisters have gone far away to white old men.
At night the sleeper found them under the columns in the
          entrance hall,
Returned from sad pilgrimages.

Oh! how their hair bristles with muck and worms,
When he steps into it with silver feet,
And they, having died, step out of bare rooms.

The passage from "Traum und Umnachtung," which uses a similar setting, reads as follows:

Chased by bats, he plunged away into the dark. Breathless, he entered the ruined house. In the courtyard he, a wild animal, drank of the well's blue waters until he became cold. Feverish, he sat on the icy stairway raging 'gainst [gen] God that he might die. Oh, the gray face of terror when he raised his round eyes over a dove's carved-up throat.

Both passages are "set"—if one can use this critical term which is appropriate to more realistic forms of literature—in the ruined family house at a point where the protagonist of each poem enters. Both poems, moreover, alternate what seem to be objective descriptions with exclamatory outbursts. But the effect of each passage is strikingly different. In "Helian," as in most of Trakl's free verse, we are aware of a slowness of movement, of processes steadily going on. The reader lingers over images; and suggestiveness takes the place of a continuous succession of events. Much of the suggestiveness in such passages comes from the pauses between the short stanzas, which, if I may refer again to Rilke's remarks on the poem, serve essentially as "a few enclosures around the boundlessly inexpressible."[3]

Quite in contrast, the passage from "Traum und Umnachtung" is notable for its lack of pauses; the paragraph from which it is taken is, in fact, some thirty lines long. Trakl sustains the violent rapidity of these lines throughout all four sections of the poem. Verbs of violent action such as "chased," "plunged," and "raging" are used constantly. The speaker seems almost breathless to unfold his narrative: short phrases, each following relentlessly upon the last, contrast strikingly with the long breath groups of "Helian." Moreover, the seemingly infinite suggestiveness that characterizes the free-verse style here gives way to an illusion of narrative completeness. Throughout this and the other prose poems, Trakl provides at least a semblance of continuity to the extent that we follow the protagonist's movements step by step, whereas in a poem such as "Helian" the poet's focus often shifts radically between one stanza and the next. Indeed, it is precisely this narrative element within "Traum and Umnachtung" which gives the poem the cohesion it needs to sustain itself throughout its great length. Despite its length, I print a complete translation, but I provide the German text only for those expressions whose English equivalent I despair of rendering adequately (the section numbers, which are not present in the original text, are added for convenience):

I

In the evening the father became an old man; in dark rooms the mother's face turned to stone and the curse of the degenerate family weighed heavily upon the boy. Sometimes he remembered his childhood, filled with sickness, terror, and darkness, secretive games in the star-garden or that he fed the rats in the dawning [darkening] courtyard. From a blue mirror there stepped out the slender form of the [his] sister and he plunged, as though dead, into the dark. At night his mouth broke open like a red fruit and the stars were [began] sparkling over his speechless grief. His dreams filled up the old house of his fathers. In the evening he liked to walk over the ruined graveyard, or he viewed the corpses in the darkening dead-room ["Totenkammer"], the green spots of corruption on their lovely hands. At the monastery gate he asked for a piece of bread; the shadow of a black horse jumped out of the dark and frightened him. When he lay in his cool bed, indescribable tears took possession of him. But there was no one who might have put his hand on his forehead. When autumn came, he walked, a clairvoyant, in [a] brown meadow. Oh the hours of wild rapture, the evenings along the green river, the hunting. Oh the soul which sang softly the song of the yellowed reed; fiery piety. Quietly and long he looked into the star-eyes of the toad, felt with shuddering hands the coolness of the old stone and conjured [away] the venerable legend of the blue spring. Oh the silver fishes and the fruits which fell from stunted trees. The chords of his strides filled him with pride and contempt of men. On the way home he came upon an uninhabited castle. Gods in ruin stood in the garden, mourning ["hintrauernd"] in the evening. But to him it seemed: here I lived forgotten years. An organ chorale filled him with God's awe. But in [a] dark cave he spent his days, lied and stole and hid, a flaming wolf, before the mother's white face. Oh the hour when with stony mouth he sank away in the star-garden, [when] the shadow of the murderer came over him. With purple forehead he walked into the moor and God's wrath punished his metal shoulders; oh the birch trees in the storm, the dark animals which avoided his benighted [deranged] paths. Hate burned away his heart, lust, when, in the flourishing summer garden, he violated the silent child, recognized his [own] benighted [deranged] face in the beaming one [the child]. Woe [for] the evening at the window, when, a gruesome skeleton, death stepped out of purple flowers. Oh you towers and bells; and the shadows of night fell stonily on him.

II

No one loved him. His head burned away falsehood and lewdness in darkening rooms. The blue rustle of a woman's dress made him stiffen to a pillar and in the door stood the nocturnal shape of his mother. At his head the shadow of evil rose up. Oh you nights and stars. In the evening he walked up the mountain with the cripple; the sunset's rosy splendor lay on the icy summit and his heart rang quietly in the twilight. The stormy fir trees sank heavily upon them and the red huntsman stepped out of the forest. When night came, his heart broke crystal-like and the darkness beat his forehead. Under bare oak trees, with icy hands, he strangled a wild cat. On his right, lamenting, the white shape of an angel appeared, and the shadow of the cripple grew larger in the dark. But he [the boy] lifted a rock and threw it at the other so that he fled howling, and in the shadow of the tree the gentle face of the angel vanished sighing. For a long time he lay on [a] rocky field and gazed, astonished, at the golden tent of the stars. Chased by bats, he plunged away into the dark. Breathless, he entered the ruined house. In the courtyard he, a wild animal, drank of the well's blue waters until he became cold. Feverish [raving], he sat on the icy stairway raging 'gainst ["gen," an archaic form] God that he might die. Oh the gray face of terror, when he raised his round eyes over a dove's carved-up throat. Slipping away over unfamiliar stairs he encountered a whore ["Judenmädchen"—which mean "Jewess," but in this context refers to a girl from the Judengasse, Salzburg's street of brothels] and he snatched at her black hair, and he seized her mouth. Hostile beings ["Feindliches"—a neuter noun] followed him through dark streets and an iron clattering tore his ear. Along autumnal walls he, an altar boy, quietly followed the silent priest; under withered trees, drunkenly, he breathed in the scarlet of his [the priest's] sacred cassock. Oh the ruined [decayed, crumbled] disk of the sun. Sweet torments devoured his flesh. In a deserted passageway ["Durchhaus," an Austrian term for a building used as a shortcut between two streets] there appeared to him, bristling with refuse, his [own] bloody shape. More deeply he loved the lofty workings of the stone; [loved] the tower which, with hellish grimaces, nightly storms the blue firmament; [loved] the cool grave, in which man's fiery heart is preserved. Woe [for] the indescribable guilt to which it [the heart] testifies. But when, intent upon something blazing ["Glühendes sinnend"—the first word being a neuter gerund] he walked down the autumnal river under bare trees, there appeared to him, in a hair shirt, a flaming daemon, the [his] sister. As he awakened, the stars at her head went out.

III

Oh the cursed family. When in defiled [polluted, bespattered] rooms, the destiny of each has been fulfilled, death, with rotting strides, steps into the house. Oh that it were spring outdoors and a lovely bird were singing in the blossoming tree. But horribly the scanty green withers on the windows of the nocturnal ones ["der Nächtlichen"] and the bleeding hearts are still meditating evil. Oh the dawning [darkening] spring paths of the contemplative ["des Sinnenden"]. More righteously he rejoices in the blossoming hedge, the countryman's green [young] crop and the singing bird, God's gentle creature; the evening bell and the beautiful community ["Gemeine"—an archaic spelling] of men. That he might forget his fate and the thorny sting. Unconfined [freely], the brook grows green where his foot wanders silver-like and an uttering tree rustles above his benighted [deranged] head. Thus, with slender hands, he lifts the snake, and in fiery tears his heart melted away. Sublime is the silence of the forest, darkness grown green ["ergrüntes Dunkel"] and the mossy animals, fluttering upward when night comes. Oh the terror, when every being knows its guilt, walks thorny paths. Thus in the brambles he found the white shape of the child, bleeding for its bridegroom's cloak. Yet he stood mute and suffering before her, buried in his steel-like hair. Oh the radiant angels, whom the purple night wind dispersed. All night he dwelled in a crystalline cave and leprosy grew silver-like on his forehead. A shadow, he walked down the mule track under autumnal stars. Snow fell, and blue darkness filled the house. [As with] a blind man, the stern [harsh] voice of the father sounded and conjured up [exorcised] terror. Woe for the bent-down coming forth ["Erscheinung"] of the women. Under stiffened hands the terrified family's food and household goods ["Frucht und Gerät"] crumbled into ruin. A wolf tore apart the firstborn and the sisters fled into dark gardens to bony old men. A benighted [deranged] seer, he sang along ruined walls and God's wind swallowed up his voice. Oh the voluptuousness of death. Oh you children of a dark breed. Silver-like the evil flowers of the blood glimmer on his temple, the cold moon in his shattered eyes. Oh [for] those of night ["der Nächtlichen"—a genitive plural]; oh [for] the cursed.

IV

Deep is the slumber in dark poisons, filled with stars and the mother's white face, the stony one [face]. Bitter is death, the fare of the guilt-laden; in the trunk's [family's] brown branches the earthen faces disintegrated grinning [sneering]. But quietly he sang in the elderberry's green shade when he awakened from bad dreams; like a sweet playfellow a rosy angel approached him, so that he, a gentle animal, slumbered away at night and he saw the star-face of purity. The sunflower sank goldlike over the garden fence when summer came. Oh the diligence of the bees and the green leaves of the walnut tree;

the thunderstorms passing by. Silver-like the poppy also bloomed, carried our nocturnal star-dreams in a green capsule. Oh how quiet the house was when the father walked away [departed] into the dark. The fruit ripened purple on the tree and the gardener busied his stern [harsh] hands; oh the sackcloth-like ["härenen," as used in the Book of Revelation] signs in the radiant sun. But quietly in the evening the shadow of the dead man entered the grieving circle of his people and his stride sounded crystal-like over the flourishing meadow before the forest. Silent ones, they gathered together at the table; dying ones, with waxen hands they broke the bread that bleeds. Woe [for] the sister's stony eyes, when, at supper, her madness passed over to the brother's nocturnal forehead, [when] the mother's bread, under suffering hands, turned to stone. Oh [for] those who have rotted ["der Verwesten"], when, with silver tongues, they held their silence about hell. Thus the lamps in the cool room died out and the suffering beings, through purple masks, looked silently at one another. All night rain rushed down and revived the meadows. In thorny wilderness the dark one followed the yellowed paths in the grain field; [followed] the song of the lark and the gentle stillness of the green branches, so that he might find peace. Oh you villages and mossy steps, blazing sight ["glühender Anblick"]. But bonily the strides tremble over sleeping snakes at the forest's edge and the ear keeps following the raving scream of the vulture. In the evening he found stony solitude, [he found] a dead man [as] escort into the dark house of the father. [A] purple cloud clouded his head so that he silently assaulted his own blood and likeness, a moonlike face; stonily he sank away into the emptiness, when in a broken mirror there appeared a dying youth, the [his] sister; the night swallowed up the cursed family.

(I, 147-50)

More fully than any other Trakl poem, "Traum und Umnach-tung" seems rooted in a real and recognizable world of everyday things. The scene is the Salzburg world of Trakl's childhood, a setting of old churches, uninhabited castles, cemeteries, winding river, and wooded mountains that actually separate parts of the city. More specifically, the poem is set in the family house, with its stairway, courtyard, and well, its food supplies and household implements. The central "characters" of the poem, if one can call them that, are members of the family—the youthful protagonist, the sister whom he violates (Section I), the aging father, the mother whose face turns to stone (I) and whose sudden confrontation of her children engaged in sexual experimentation (II) shocks the reader with the sort of narrative force he does not expect in poetry. The sentence "No one loved him," with which the second section opens, could, in fact, come out of most any piece of modern fiction, yet "Traum und Umnachtung," in its range of reference and its mode of organization, seems as far removed from fiction as any work could be. As in Trakl's free verse, though in a far more conspicuous way, we have the semblance of narrative without the unfolding of any narrative in the usual sense of the word.

The poem is built around the protagonist's wanderings in and about Salzburg—within the house, to the river, up a mountain, along the streets. His wanderings, one might say, are the particular events out of which the poem's larger meanings must be read. We follow him in his obsessive wanderings to the scene of his crime (III); in his penitential wanderings through "thorny" places (IV); in his search for grace as he follows the priest to "breathe in the scarlet of his sacred cassock" (II). "He walked . . . he followed . . . he plunged"—subject-verb combinations such as these shape the action of the poem throughout. Thus, outward event becomes the symbol and indicator of inward process.

The poem is built not only out of the boy's wanderings but also out of sudden appearances, entrances, intrusions: the mother standing at the boy's door (II); death (in the shape of a "gruesome skelton," as though stepping out of a medieval allegory) emerging from a bed of purple flowers (I); the sister confronting the boy as she steps out of the mirror (I) or stands before him in a hair shirt (II); and, perhaps most memorable of all, the image, described as "bleeding" and "bristling with refuse," which he suddenly recognizes as his own (II).

Events follow one another with a rapidity and an apparent lack of logical connection which can be explained in one sense by the word "dream" in the poem's title, but whose only adequate analogy is perhaps the avant-garde film of recent years. And like the contemporary film, the poem moves back and forth, unself-consciously, between the real and the fantastic, and among disparate objects which are glimpsed only momentarily. Trakl strains language to the utmost to achieve a sense of constant movement. The present participle form, much rarer in German than in English, is used frequently: death enters with "rotting" ("modernde") strides (III); the protagonist is "raging" ("rasend") against God (II). Adverbs and adverbial phrases are used to begin an uncommon number of sentences, as though Trakl were bent on constantly keeping the reader in suspense: "horribly . . . withers" (III); "more righteously he rejoices" (III); "silver-like . . . bloomed" (IV). Abstractions are kept to a minimum: the overpowering effect of the word "grief" in the line "The stars were sparkling over his speechless grief" (I) comes from the con-creteness of the context in which the word is embedded; by the same token, the allegorical death who steps into the family house (III) exercises a power over the modern reader through the concreteness with which the ruined household has been made real to him in the preceding pages.

As in all of Trakl's verse from "Helian" onward, the most incongruous categories are fused together: "strides" is qualified by "rotting" (III), "mouth" by "stony" (I), "face" by "moonlike" (IV). The effect of such incongruities is that the poem creates a verbal universe of its own independent of the reader's everyday world. Our normal conceptions of time and space, moreover, are constantly jarred, as in the following succession of sentences: "His head burned away falsehood and lewdness in darkening rooms. The blue rustle of a woman's dress made him stiffen to a pillar and in the door stood the nocturnal shape of his mother" (II). Although all the verbs remain in the narrative past, we sense conflicting levels of time. The first sentence implies a series of events that took place a number of times in a number of different rooms. The second sentence presents a specific event occurring at a single time and place. By jumbling categories in this way, Trakl is able not only to assert the autonomy of the world of the poem, but also to distance himself, as it were, from realities ("lewdness in darkening rooms") which are too painful to render in conventional narrative terms.

One of many such distancing devices in the poem is the representation of individual characters in a multiple number of roles. Thus, as in "Helian" and other Trakl poems, the protag-onist of "Traum und Umnachtung" appears in a number of guises; he is variously described as altar boy (II), clairvoyant (I), mad prophet (III), "dark one" (IV), gentle animal (IV), contemplative (III), and is shown in such stances as beggar (I), rapist (I), and sadist (II). The sister, in her turn, is variously an innocent victim (I and III) and a mad-woman (IV), and at one climatic point she is described as a "flaming daemon" in penitent's clothing (II). The ease with which characters shift from one guise to another becomes all the more evident when we look at Trakl's manuscript changes: in one place he altered the word "sister" to read "caretaker's daughter" ("Hausmeisters-tochter") and then back to "sister" again (*see* critical edition, II, 265); in much the same way the protagonist's guise as clair-voyant had taken the form of "a fallen angel" ("ein gefallener Engel") in an earlier version (*see* II, 266).

But the conventional terminology of fiction and drama is inadequate for works such as this; rather than speak of "guises," one must see the "characters" as analogous, complementary even, to one another. The rapist is the other side of the coin from the prophet. The cripple who accompanies the boy up the mountain in the second section represents his pitiable, distorted aspect; the "red huntsman," his lustful side. Even brother and sister are in a sense analogues to one another, as Trakl suggests obliquely through the image of the mirror, by means of which the sister confronts the brother at the beginning and at the end of the poem.

The mirror image, moreover, hints at the insubstantiality of the various "characters." A person's image, one might say, is rendered less substantial through its being viewed in a mirror; by something of the same process, the characters come to seem less substantial, less autonomous, through such terms as "figure" ("Gestalt"), "face" ("Antlitz"), and "shadow" ("Schatten") which Trakl attaches to them repeatedly in the poem. We are shown the *figure*, or *shape*, of the sister (I and III), of an angel (II), of the mother (II); the *face* of the mother (I and IV), of the angel (II), of terror (II) and purity (IV), and of the pro-tagonist himself (IV); the *shadow* of a horse (I), of the cripple (II), and also of the protagonist (III).

Just as characters are constantly being fragmented, so they can also merge. By the end of the poem, as the family goes to its common doom, all, in one sense, become analogues to one another. The protagonist's role might best be described in the terms used by T. S. Eliot of his "character" Tiresias in *The Waste Land* (a poem grounded in much the same esthetic as Trakl's). Tiresias, Eliot tells us in his notes, "unites all the rest" of the personages of the poem: "Just as the one-eyed merchant, seller of currants, melts into the Phoenician Sailor, and the latter is not wholly distinct from Ferdinand Prince of Naples, so all the women are one woman, and the two sexes meet in Tiresias. What Tiresias *sees*, in fact, is the substance of the poem."[4] Eliot's statement reflects the difficulty of speaking of characters in post-Symbolist literature in conventional terms. The English poet bypasses, as it were, the limitations in his critical vocabulary by employing words such as "unites," "melts," and "meet" to indicate the analogous relationships among his "characters."

Traditional conceptions of plot are as inapplicable to "Traum und Umnachtung" as are traditional conceptions of character. Despite its wealth of narrative elements, the poem avoids the chronological development and cause-and-effect relationships which we normally associate with narrative. Given only the evidence which the poem itself presents, one cannot even say that the protagonist's relation to his sister was the "cause" of his guilt and madness. Rather, his guilt and madness are inherent features of the family and its setting, which are characterized from the start by words such as "degenerated," "fallen," and "ruined."

Yet the poem follows a regular movement, a movement determined not by "plot" but by the alternation of contrary states of the mind. As in many of his poems in free verse, Trakl achieves dramatic tension by juxtaposing scenes of loveliness with the most hellish of visions. In "Traum und Umnachtung" he often effects his transitions with the word "but" ("aber" in German), a device which, like many others in his later work, he borrowed from Hölderlin, who used it constantly to indicate dialectical shifts of direction.[5] To cite a single example in Trakl's poem, note the rapid transition from demonic to idyllic between the second and the third sentences of the fourth section: "In the trunk's brown branches their earthen faces disintegrated grinning. *But* quietly he sang in the elderberry's green shade, when he awakened from bad dreams."

In view of the mode of organization he employed, Trakl might conceivably have kept the poem going indefinitely, alternating positive and negative states with persistent regularity. The only way to bring it to a conclusion was through some blinding celestial vision or some uncompromising depiction of doom which would outdo the effect of any of the previous images. Trakl chose the latter course. In the final words, the family is swallowed up with something of the abject horror with which the hell-jaw contraption of the medieval stage sent its victims to the infernal depths. The German text of these words, "Die Nacht das verfluchte Geschlecht verschlang," with its dislocated syntax and its piling up of back vowels and sounds such as *cht* and *schl,* achieves a bravura effect which sounds the note of doom in a way that no translation can approximate.

Yet this note of doom is anticipated throughout the final section. The alternations between positive and negative states take place with greater frequency and with a more frantic tone than anywhere else in the poem. The family meal which Trakl depicts here achieves an uncommon power through our recognition that it is, in effect, a parody of the Last Supper. The "silent ones" who "gather together at the table" experience a communion that is notable for its demonic rather than its spiritual qualities. The sister infects the brother with her madness, and the mother's bread turns to stone in her hand, as though in mockery of the communion and in answer to the question posed in the Gospels, "O what man is there of you, whom if his son ask bread, will he give him a stone?" (Matthew 7:9). The ultimate irony of Trakl's supper scene is that the members of the doomed family are so incapable of verbal contact that they force themselves to suppress the hell which is on their tongues.

The reader, in retrospect, remains aware perhaps only of the dominant note of doom. But, throughout the poem, Trakl is at pains to find words and images which look in positive and negative directions at once; it is as though he seeks to maintain a sense of uncertainty as to which direction he wants the poem to take. The "sweet torments" which "devoured" the protagonist's flesh are both a punishment of unspeakable crime and a sign of relationship to God (II). Trakl's ambiguity is of course deeply rooted within Christian tradition. The recurrent images of stone, crystal, and bone are also used in what might seem contradictory contexts. On one level we see the mother's face (I) and her bread (IV) turn to stone and the protagonist sink "stonily" into emptiness (IV), but we also note that the boy seeks solace in "the coolness of the old stone" (I) and "loved the sublime workings of the stone" (II). The reader can understand the meaning of such images only by a kind of intuition: stone is deathlike, dehumanizing, but it is also stable, coolly refreshing, mysterious, inwardly austere, and ultimately unknowable; like bone, it can be brittle, break apart, decompose, become the earth out of which new life perhaps can sprout.

The richest concept within the poem is darkness and night, for which Trakl employs a variety of words—"dunkel" ("dark"),

"dämmern" (which can mean either 'to dawn" or "grow dusk"),
"Nacht" ("night"), and "Finsternis" ('darkness" in its blackest
and gloomiest form). The word "night" alone is forced into a
number of derivatives: the family is called "die Nächtlichen"
("the nocturnal ones" [III]); the mother's shape as she stands
in the boy's door is "nächtig" ("of night" [II]). The word
"Umnachtung" in the poem's title can only partially be rendered
by the English word "madness." "Umnachtung" means also
"being surrounded by night," and it is used several times in the
poem in both these senses; at one point, for instance, the protagonist is "ein unnachteter Seher," a "be-nighted prophet (III).
Madness in the poem serves both as a punishment and as an
escape from terror. Night, in turn, is both a time of renewal,
as when rain revives the meadow (IV), and the infernal instrument which swallows up the family in the final line.

The negative forces in the poem play so powerful a role that
Trakl had to develop a variety of verbal devices to give the
positive elements sufficient weight. Sometimes he relies on the
evocative effect of nature images, as in the "diligence of the
bees and the green leaves of the walnut tree" (IV). Sometimes
he resorts to new word compounds, most notably words built
out of "star": "Sternenantlitz der Reinheit" ("star-face of purity"
[IV]); "Sternengarten" ("star-garden" [I]); "Sternenträume"
("star-dreams" [IV]). At one point (II), when he introduces
an angel, he lets it appear with the sort of casualness one
associates with the entrances of angels in medieval morality
plays. At another point (III) he presents a series of biblical-
pastoral images reminiscent of those in "Ein Winterabend" and
the third section of "Helian." The phrase "more righteously he
rejoices in . . ." (III) echoes a Psalm (33:1) in Luther's translation, and the images that follow—"the countryman . . . the
singing bird, God's gentle creature . . . the evening bell and the
beautiful community of men" (for "community" he employed an
obviously archaic form, "Gemeine") all suggest a traditional,
custom-rooted society.

But close attention to the text often reveals the precariousness
of these positive visions. One of these, for example, is introduced
by verbs in the subjunctive, "Oh that it were spring outdoors and
a lovely bird were singing in the blossoming tree" (III); by means
of the subjunctive Trakl is able to stress the loveliness and its
make-believe quality at the same time. When the "nocturnal star-

dreams," moreover, are admitted to be the result of opium (presented graphically in its "green capsule" [IV]), the apparently "positive" dreams are unmasked as the product of an artificial paradise. The whole poem, for that matter, could be interpreted as a single long opium dream.

The autobiographical elements of the poem—the incest, the opium, the meticulously detailed Salzburg setting—are so prominent that critics have approached the poem principally from a biographical point of view. Even if Trakl had retained his original title, "Der Untergang Kaspar Münchs" ("The Fall of Kaspar Münch" [*see* II, 265]), the autobiographical element would have revealed itself easily through the persona he assumed. It seems no accident that one of the earliest biographical studies, as well as the most recent one, quotes from "Traum und Umnachtung" more than from any other poem.[6] Yet the poem's strongly autobiographical content can all too easily narrow down the frame of reference through which the reader is likely to view the poem. It seems to me less significant that "Traum und Umnachtung" happens to reveal something of Trakl's childhood life than that the poem succeeds in setting his private experiences within a larger tragic perspective. Events which, in other contexts, might have seemed trivial or lurid or pathetic, are here endowed with an aura of cosmic significance. The details of family life are only a single dimension within which the poem operates. The world which the poem creates contains polarities of the most diverse kind: naturalistic domestic detail ("food and household goods" [III]) and the intercession of angels (II and IV); macabre grotesquery ("the earthen faces disintegrated grinning" [IV]) and the showing forth of divine light ("and gazed, astonished, at the golden tent of the stars" [II]); simple descriptive statement ("in the evening he walked up the mountain with the cripple" [II]) and the language of what an earlier century would have called the "high" style ("night swallowed up the cursed family" [IV]).

Behind this vast machinery the poem is motivated, throughout, by a central moral drama of guilt and repentance, of compulsion toward crime and longing for grace. Trakl's description of the purpose of his poetry as "incomplete atonement" (I, 463), can be applied in a more rigorous way to "Traum and Umnachtung" than to any other of his poems. The overt personal impulses that generate the poem and are embodied in its complex lyrical

structure, produce what seems like the essence of tragic experience; yet, through the extreme compression of Trakl's Symbolist
method, the tragic experience is rendered in spatial rather than
temporal terms. To put it another way, Trakl has approached the
tragic mode without having to follow the neatly ordered linear
development characterized by the Aristotelian concept of
dramatic action. Through its implied drama, its narrative prose,
and its lyrical language, the form which Trakl created in "Traum
und Umnachtung" comes about as close to fusing the major
genres as any work conceivably can.

Unique though it seems, the poem also has distinct roots within
literary tradition. Its most direct literary ancestor is Rimbaud's
Une Saison en Enfer, to which its feverish visionary prose is
closely akin. Trakl's obsession with the family as the source of
(or analogue to) his protagonist's damnation parallels Rimbaud's
treatment of his family in that section of his poem entitled
"Mauvais Sang" ("Bad Blood"). One might add that Trakl
refers to the family, not with the everyday term "Familie," but
with the word "Geschlecht," which encompasses such meanings
as race, stock, generation, sex, and species; like Rimbaud, he
implicitly extends his frame of reference from the individual
family to mankind as a whole. Throughout the poem, again like
Rimbaud, he stresses his protagonist's alienation from family and
community, as well as his violence, typified in each poem through
his portrayal as a "wild animal."[7]

But *Une Saison en Enfer* is relevant to "Traum und Umnachtung" less in its individual details than in its larger thematic
statements and in the example it sets of an extensive poetic
structure written in prose. Rimbaud, as I indicated earlier, had
already exercised his most decisive influence on Trakl in the
period between "Psalm" and "Helian," more than a year before
the writing of "Traum und Umnachtung." Within the total curve
of Trakl's development, that side of Rimbaud which helped
give shape to "Helian" presides, as it were, over his work of the
succeeding year: in its lyricism and its elegiac slowness of movement, the style of "Helian" anticipates such poems of 1913 as
"Elis" and "Am Mönchsberg." Similarly, the demonic side of
Rimbaud which manifests itself in "Traum und Umnachtung"
anticipates much that is characteristic of the poems of Trakl's
final year. In its dramatic tensions, its predominant note of doom,
its infernal grandeur, "Traum und Umnachtung" looks forward

to such characteristic poems of 1914 as the final version of "Abendland" ("Occident" or "Evening-Land" [I, 139-40]), "Das Gewitter," and "Offenbarung und Untergang."

If "Helian" and "Traum und Umnachtung" thus point to different directions in Trakl's development, they are also significant
as his most successful attempts to create a poetic structure more
extensive than that of the short lyric. Through their largeness
of vision and their accumulation of detail they seem poems of
a different kind from his short lyrics, despite the fact that these
lyrics employ the same images, tones, and techniques as the
longer poems. By means of the Symbolist method which Trakl
used, both of these poems, moreover, seem longer and more
comprehensive in scope than one would think possible of a poem
of less than a hundred lines such as "Helian," or of the four
pages which "Traum und Umnachtung" occupies in the critical
edition. One could, in fact, sketch a tradition of Symbolist "long"
poems to which these poems belong: it would include such
works as *Une Saison en Enfer, The Waste Land, The Bridge,*
and the *Duino Elegies,* which, like the much longer long poems
of the past, create the illusion that they encompass a large cycle
of human experience and can build their own autonomous
worlds.[8] Trakl's commentators tend to locate his greatness either
in the uniqueness of his work as a whole or in his mastery of
the short lyric,[9] but it may well be that in the future his longer
poems—"Helian" and "Traum und Umnachtung," as well as
"Offenbarung und Untergang"[10]—will come to seem his central
contribution to the history of German poetry.

II   "Das Gewitter"

The feverish, demonic prose of "Traum und Umnachtung" did
not find an adequate equivalent in Trakl's verse style until several
months after its completion. The development of this new form
of verse, which occurred in the spring of 1914, represents a
stylistic breakthrough almost as spectacular and thoroughgoing
as Trakl's earlier development of a free-verse style in "Psalm"
and "Helian." This breakthrough can be charted in detail
through a study of the numerous manuscript changes of the
poem "Abendland" between its original composition in March,
1914, and its final version, which was completed by early June
(*see* I, 139-40, 399-410, and II, 241-58). Since an adequate study

of "Abendland" would take me well beyond the confines of this
book (the second of its four versions is more than half again as
long as "Helian"), I shall look instead at "Das Gewitter," one
of a group of seven poems[11] which reveal Trakl's new style in
its fully developed phase:

> Ihr wilden Gebirge, der Adler
> Erhabene Trauer.
> Goldnes Gewölk
> Raucht über steinerner Öde.
> Geduldige Stille odmen die Föhren,
> Die schwarzen Lämmer am Abgrund,
> Wo plötzlich die Bläue
> Seltsam verstummt,
> Das sanfte Summen der Hummeln.
> O grüne Blume—
> O Schweigen.
>
> Traumhaft erschüttern des Wildbachs
> Dunkle Geister das Herz,
> Finsternis,
> Die über die Schluchten hereinbricht!
> Weisse Stimmen
> Irrend durch schaurige Vorhöfe,
> Zerrissne Terrassen,
> Der Väter gewaltiger Groll, die Klage
> Der Mütter,
> Des Knaben goldener Kriegsschrei
> Und Ungebornes
> Seufzend aus blinden Augen.
>
> O Schmerz, du flammendes Anschaun
> Der grossen Seele!
> Schon zuckt im schwarzen Gewühl
> Der Rosse und Wagen
> Ein rosenschauriger Blitz
> In die tönende Fichte.
> Magnetische Kühle
> Umschwebt dies stolze Haupt,
> Glühende Schwermut
> Eines zürnenden Gottes.
>
> Angst, du giftige Schlange,
> Schwarze, stirb im Gestein!
> Da stürzen der Tränen

Wilde Ströme herab,
Sturm-Erbarmen,
Hallen in drohenden Donnern
Die schneeigen Gipfel rings.
Feuer
Läutert zerrissene Nacht.

1 You savage mountains, the eagles'
2 Sublime grief.
3 Golden cloud mass
4 Smokes over stony waste.
5 Patient stillness is breathed by the firs,
6 [By] the black lambs at the abyss,
7 Where suddenly the blueness
8 Strangely turns mute,
9 The soft droning of the bumblebees.
10 O green flower—
11 O silence.

12 Dreamlike the torrent's
13 Dark spirits shatter the heart,
14 Darkness,
15 Which breaks in upon the gorges!
16 White voices
17 Straying through horrible [shuddering] vestibules,
18 Torn terraces,
19 The fathers' violent rancor, the lament
20 Of the mothers,
21 The boy's golden war cry
22 And unborn [neuter noun]
23 Groaning out of blind eyes.

24 O pain, you flaming vision
25 Of the great [vast] soul!
26 Already, in the black tumult
27 Of the steeds and carriages
28 A rose-showering [rose-shuddering] lightning bolt
29 Flashes into the sounding spruce.
30 Magnetic coolness
31 Floats around this proud head,
32 Glowing melancholy
33 Of a wrathful God.

34 Fear, you poisonous snake,
35 Black one, die among the stones!

36   Then [there] the tears'
37   Wild rivers plunge downward,
38   Storm-compassion,
39   Resound in menacing thunders
40   Around the snowy peaks.
41   Fire
42   Purifies torn night.

(I, 157-58)

The slow-moving elegiac lines of poems such as "Helian" and "Elis" here give way to short, often abrupt lines that move with an unrelenting force similar to the prose of "Traum und Umnachtung." Verbs such as "convulse," "plunge," "flash," and adjectives such as "torn" and "shuddering" (each used twice) define the nature of the poem. Indeed, the lines "where suddenly the blueness / Strangely turns mute" of the first stanza could be taken as an emblem of Trakl's shift from the blue night world of many earlier poems of 1913 to the unpredictable and tersely expressed changes that occur within his poems after "Abendland."

From "Helian" onward, and certainly throughout 1913, Trakl created the illusion of a world fully independent of the observable world familiar to the reader. The dying animals, the small boats floating downstream, the sister appearing at night as a vision in the sky, and even the ruined furniture in the family home— all these images, though each can be related, in one way or another, to the observable world, seem part of a coherent and structured world of their own, which we view as though through a glass or in a dream. In "Das Gewitter," Trakl's private world no longer manifests this autonomy and continuity. The observable world, which in this poem takes the shape of mountain peaks and gorges, is inextricably mixed with images from Trakl's private world: a green flower, lamentations by members of the family, or a wrathful god's glowing melancholy. Tenor and vehicle become indiscernible from one another: are the "white voices" in the mountain gorge symbols for the family's laments, or are these laments introduced to define the sounds of the storm? Both of these interpretations are equally plausible.

We are conscious, moreover, that individual aspects of the scene are "real" and metaphorical at once. The abyss in line 6 is both an observable part of the mountain and a symbol of the precariousness to which the lambs, whose blackness suggests a kind of tarnished innocence, are exposed. The wild rivers of the final stanza are, in one sense, a part of the natural scene, but they are introduced as the "tears' wild rivers," as though to suggest that the mountain setting is analogous to a psychological setting which must ultimately remain undefined. By contrast, the Salzburg landscape depicted in "Am Mönchsberg" had little reality of its own, or, to put it differently, the actual landscape has been fully absorbed by the mental landscape which dominates the poem. In the earlier poems, every image is a metaphor of sorts, but we accept these metaphors as the only reality within the poem. In "Das Gewitter," on the other hand, the real mountains and the real thunderstorms are able to retain their identity against the pressures of a strange mixture of alien worlds.[12]

This mixture is evident, for instance, in Trakl's fusion of images drawn from seemingly diverse contexts. In the third stanza, for example, the lightning bolt, which is part of the poem's most literal level of meaning, emerges from a "tumult of steeds and carriages," a characteristically "literary" image which one might expect to find, say, in a Goethe or a Schiller ballad. The mountain gorges contain "vestibules" or "porches," images drawn from architecture. In fact, it is impossible to suggest any meaningful relationships between the various contexts from which Trakl draws his images.

Throughout the poem, moreover, Trakl ruthlessly mixes categories and contexts in order to achieve the most dissonant possible effects. The highly concrete mountain landscape (so concrete, in fact, that after Trakl's death Ludwig von Ficker used to point out the actual setting—at the edge of Innsbruck—to visitors) is balanced against a far larger number of abstractions than one normally finds in Trakl's verse. "Glowing melancholy" is, to be sure, a typical Trakl abstraction in the sense that it gains concreteness through the adjective preceding it. But "pain" and "fear" are both invoked at conspicuous moments (ll. 24 and 34) without preceding modifiers and are allegorized only afterward. Violent opposites are pitted against one another. Darkness is interrupted by the "actual" lightning bolt and by images of "glowing" and "flaming." Silence, invoked at the end of the first stanza, is set against the varied and powerful sounds of the storm.

In contrast to the precise and often small objects out of which the earlier poems are constructed, "Das Gewitter" is notable for the sense of largeness which dominates it throughout. For example, the poem is full of collective nouns—"Gewölk" ("cloud mass"), "Gewühl" ("tumult"), "Gebirge" ("mountains"), "Gestein" ("stone mass"), all of which demonstrate their collective status in German through the prefix *Ge*. Although in the earlier poems the father and the mother generally appear in the singular, here, as though to create an unreal and massive effect, they appear in the plural. The majority of the concrete nouns, in fact, are plural: "terraces," "vestibules," ' 'rivers," "gorges," "thunders," "summits." The "literal" meaning of the poem would be scarcely different if these words were in the singular, but the sense of overwhelming power they generate would somehow be lessened.

Throughout most of his work, from the early rhymed verse through the free verse of 1913, Trakl's characteristic rhetorical mode was descriptive. Although invocations often interrupted the descriptions, they rarely threatened to dominate the poem. "Das Gewitter," together with the other poems composed during the same period, represents a significant shift from the descriptive to the vocative mode. It is as though the power he wishes to unleash could be expressed verbally only by means of confrontation and invocation. A few earlier poems, certainly, were written in the second person. But the uses to which Trakl puts the second person in "Das Gewitter" are radically different from those of earlier poems. The second person in "An den Knaben Elis," for instance, was used to express a longing for a lost state of innocence, and in several poems addressed to his sister —for instance, "An die Schwester" (To the [My] Sister") and "Abendlied" ("Evening Song"), both of which were part of the so-called " 'Helian'-complex"—it became a means of evoking a state of tender and intimate relationship.

The second person of "Das Gewitter," on the other hand, is used to confront and exorcise. In the course of the poem, the speaker successively addresses the mountain range, the green flower, silence, pain, and fear. The descriptive passages interwoven among the invocations are depictions either of violent action or of a kind of potential violence suggested by words such as "rancor," "groaning," and "wrathful." If the poem has any development in the conventional sense, one could say that it moves from the ominous silences of the first stanza through the noisy confusion of the second, thence to the outward show of violence by means of lightning in the third, and finally to a purification by fire in the final lines. The poem could, in fact,

be defined as the history of a mood, progressing, as it does,
from the sinister calm of the opening through the emotional
release effected by the lightning at the end. Violence, which
in most Trakl contexts has predominantly negative meanings,
here becomes the instrument for psychological catharsis.

Trakl, to be sure, had attempted something of the same
resolution in a poem written four years before. The earlier poem,
"Der Gewitterabend" ("The Evening Thunderstorm") is a
rhymed poem in his "merry-go-round" manner. Totally impersonal, it consists of the usual series of random, third-person
observations that are connected only through the theme of the
thunderstorm. In the final stanza of this poem written in 1910,
Trakl strives for an effect of exorcism that parallels the ending
of the later poem:

> Kranke kreischen im Spitale.
> Bläulich schwirrt der Nacht Gefieder.
> Glitzernd braust mit einem Male
> Regen auf die Dächer nieder.

> Sick people shriek in the hospital.   a
> Bluely the night's plumage whirs.   b
> All at once, glistening, rain bursts   a
> Down upon the roofs.   b

(I, 27)

Here Trakl relies altogether on the purgative effect of the rain
to give the poem a conclusion. As in the later poem, a sense
of violence is implicit throughout, yet this violence is "contained,"
as it were, by the strict metrical form and the impersonal stance
that govern Trakl's method of composition. The later poem, by
contrast, is built on a far vaster scale and, by virtue of its freer
mode of composition, evokes a much larger range of meanings.

The differences between these two poems, both of them on
a similar theme and with similar conclusions, suggest the extent
of Trakl's stylistic development during the relatively short period
of time which encompasses his career. Moreover, his stylistic
evolution from "Helian" to "Das Gewitter" is almost as great
as that from the early rhymed poems to the free verse of 1913.
Since the scarcely more than half-dozen poems which Trakl
completed after June, 1914, are partly in his new style, and
partly reversions to his earlier free verse, one cannot guess the
directions his poetry might have taken if he had lived longer.

But if Trakl had continued to write in the mode of the spring, 1914, poems, his work would doubtless have displayed a greater kinship with that of his Expressionist contemporaries than it actually does. In its loudness of utterance and in the dynamic nature of the speaker's stance, a poem such as "Das Gewitter" can be analyzed as a "typical" Expressionist poem much more comfortably than any of Trakl's earlier free verse, which, with its relative passivity of stance, its quietness, and its slowness of movement, superficially, at least, shares little with the work of such contemporaries as Ernst Stadler and August Stramm. Yet I can find no significant evidence of outward influence—comparable, that is, to the influence of Rimbaud on his first attempts at free verse—by any of his contemporaries on the poems of spring, 1914.[13] As a study of the genesis of "Abendland" would show, the language Trakl developed to express violence in these poems is essentially a natural development of the language of the preceding period, in which violence is often only barely contained beneath the quiet, elegiac surface.

III   *"Grodek" and "Klage"*

On the basis of "Grodek" alone, Trakl has achieved a place among the poets of World War I. The title of the poem refers to a town in Galicia (in Austrian-occupied Poland) that formed the center of a battle line during one of the earliest engagements of the war. As a result of this engagement, fought in late August and early September, 1914, the Austrians suffered a major defeat from the invading Russian army. Grodek, as it turned out, was the closest that Trakl ever got to the battlefield. His own experiences—caring for ninety seriously wounded men in a barn, watching one of them blow his brains out, walking outside to see some of the local citizenry hanging from trees—doubtless confirmed all the most demonic visions of reality that his own earlier poetry had tried to record. It seems remarkable, however, that this poem, which, with its companion piece, "Klage"—a less ambitious, though more fully realized poem—was, according to Trakl, written "at the front,"[14] has almost completely absorbed its images of ugliness and horror within a larger lyrical framework:

Am Abend tönen die herbstlichen Wälder
Von tödlichen Waffen, die goldnen Ebenen
Und blauen Seen, darüber die Sonne

Düstrer hinrollt; umfängt die Nacht
Sterbende Krieger, die wilde Klage
Ihrer zerbrochenen Münder.
Doch stille sammelt im Weidengrund
Rotes Gewölk, darin ein zürnender Gott wohnt
Das vergossne Blut sich, mondne Kühle;
Alle Strassen münden in schwarze Verwesung.
Unter goldnem Gezweig der Nacht und Sternen
Es schwankt der Schwester Schatten durch den schweigenden
        Hain,
Zu grüssen die Geister der Helden, die blutenden Häupter;
Und leise tönen im Rohr die dunkeln Flöten des Herbstes.
O stolzere Trauer! ihr ehernen Altäre
Die heisse Flamme des Geistes nährt heute ein gewaltiger
        Schmerz,
Die ungebornen Enkel.

```
 1   In the evening the autumnal woods resound
 2   With deadly arms, [as do] the golden plains
 3   And blue lakes, over which the sun
 4   Darkly [gloomily] revolves; the night embraces
 5   Dying warriors, the wild lamenting
 6   Of their broken mouths.
 7   Yet quietly in the [low] pasture there gather
 8   Red clouds, in which a wrathful god lives,
 9   The spilt blood, moonlike coolness;
10   All streets run into black decay.
11   Under golden branches of night and stars
12   The sister's shadow hovers through the silent grove
13   To greet the spirits of the heroes, the bleeding heads;
14   And softly in the reeds the dark flutes of autumn resound.
15   Oh prouder mourning! You brazen altars,
16   Today the hot flame of the spirit is fed by an immense pain,
17   The unborn grandchildren.
```
                                            (I, 167)

The poem stands at a kind of meeting point between Trakl's private poetic world—with its autumnal woods and the sister as a supernatural vision—and the pressures of outward, public event. Except for those images which Trakl drew from the Salzburg world of his childhood, the world of actual places and events rarely played any role in his poetry. Even "Menschheit," his powerful "war" poem of 1912, was, like many other poems of that period, about a war which could be conceived of solely in the imagination. The poem entitled "In Venedig" ("In Venice" [I, 131]), which commemorates the trip he took to Venice with Loos and Kraus in August, 1913, contains perhaps less evocation of place—one finds only a fleeting reference to sea and canal—than any of the innumerable poems and prose passages about Venice in German literature. Even in "Grodek" the images of war are so generalized that it could refer as easily to a battle of the ancient world as to the one during which Trakl actually composed it. For that matter, the poem's most specific images of war—the "wild lamenting" and "broken mouths" of the warriors, the red cloud mass—can be found scattered in various combinations throughout his poetry.

Quite in contrast to such English poets of the war as Wilfred Owen and Siegfried Sassoon, Trakl makes no attempt to capture the particulars of modern war. In fact, he seems always at pains to keep these particulars at a distance.[15] It is significant, for instance, that the most concrete images of war appear in apposition to relatively generalized images: the "spilt blood" is mentioned only after the generalized "red cloud"; the "bleeding heads" only after the "spirit of heroes." It is as though he dare lead up only gradually to such particulars. Moreover, Trakl chooses a relatively formal word for heads—"Häupter" instead of "Köpfe" —as if to guard against too startlingly realistic an effect. The "dying warriors" and their "wild lamenting" are literally embraced by the night, as though such horrors must be absorbed, as it were, by the permanent forms of nature.

By thus "absorbing" realistic detail within a larger perspective, Trakl achieves something of the decorum which we generally associate with tragedy. The word "tragedy" is, for the most part, inappropriate to a discussion of Trakl's poetry, which works primarily in a mythical rather than a tragic mode. Only in those poems with a strongly realistic content does he attain a tragic effect—for instance, in "Traum und Umnachtung," in which concrete images of domestic horror are balanced against pastoral and religious imagery. In "Grodek" the realistic element is less overtly expressed than in "Traum und Umnachtung," for Trakl depends, to a large degree, on the associations which the reader brings to the title. Throughout the poem, in fact, the reader's sense of the actuality of war is constantly subdued by the lofty perspectives Trakl creates through his pastoral setting and elegiac tone.

Yet "Grodek" is also characterized by a sharply dramatic quality reminiscent, in many ways, of the dramatic development I noted earlier in "Menschheit." The frequent pauses which interrupt and deliberately slow down most of his earlier poems are eliminated for the purpose of achieving a swift, closely connected series of progressions. The poem develops by dramatic intensification, with each of its four sentences defining a new and more widely encompassing point of view through which the battle may be interpreted.

In the first sentence, despite the ominous aspects of the sun, the pastoral vision has the upper hand. Night "embraces" the warriors, and the deadly weapons are almost absorbed by the autumnal woods. If these first six lines had been printed as a separate poem, one might have described "Grodek" as a poem about the process of transformation from a "negative" to a "positive" vision. The word "doch" ("yet"), which opens the second section, indicates a shift of direction. Despite the "moonlike coolness," which acts to subdue the image of "spilt blood" and of a "wrathful god"—perhaps an emblem of Mars—emphasis here is on the negative aspect of the scene. Above all, the bold image of streets running into decay creates a sense of impending cataclysm at the end of this section.

Yet the beautiful pastoral world of the next section (ll. 11-14) indicates a new, apparently higher level of awareness. Except for the "bleeding heads," nothing remains of the realities of war. Through the long, almost dactylic lines and the highly conspicuous alliteration—four *sch* sounds in line 12, two initial *g*'s and two *h*'s in the next line—Trakl evokes momentarily the heroic world of Germanic alliterative poetry, or, more precisely, Richard Wagner's attempt in the mid-nineteenth century to revive this world. The Wagnerian effect of these lines is evident not only in the meter and the alliteration, but in the sister's Valkyrie-like role as she ministers to the spirits of the dead warriors. (One might note that Trakl was fascinated by Wagner's idealization of brother-sister incest in *Die Walküre*;[16] his portrait of his own sister thus includes both Sieglinde and Brünnhilde.) In the final line of this section, Trakl indicates the great distance which the poem has encompassed from its opening line; the word "tönen" ("resound"), which had earlier been used of the "deadly weapons," now refers to the music of the reeds in the wind, as if to show the transformation of battle noises into a higher though still mournful music.

But if the poem had ended here, the final effect, with its overwrought Wagnerian pathos, would have seemed grossly sentimental. The pastoral vision and the flowing musicality of the lines are much too easily earned, and, as a result, Trakl here comes closer to a lapse of taste than perhaps anywhere in his work after "Psalm." The poem retrieves itself only by virtue of a new perspective which Trakl introduces at this point. The exclamation in line 15 indicates a shift from description to invocation. The comparative form "prouder" suggests, in turn, a more sharply intensified level of awareness. The "brazen altars" and "hot flame of the spirit" belong to a world distinctly beyond the pastoral. The sufferings of war are raised to a cosmic level as they feed the spiritual flame; it is as though the sight of human slaughter is bearable only if seen in both its horror and its grandeur at once.

It seems useless, one might add, to ask whether the final line stands in apposition to "pain" or to "flame," or whether it simply has no syntactical relationship with the preceding line. In an early, lost version of the poem, Trakl is known to have developed the image of the grandchildren for an additional two or three lines (see II, 311). The cryptic effect of this image in the final version makes the poem seem to turn upon itself: the easy fluency of the preceding lines—the third section in particular— now breaks down in the face of the poet's inability to speak under the pressure of new awareness. Between the word "today" and the image of the grandchildren in the last line, Trakl introduces a temporal perspective which he had thus far ignored: the present sufferings are only the beginning of a doom which refuses ever to be final.

Yet the negative effect of these final images is perhaps only apparent. The fact that grief can be invoked and that spiritual flames can be lit upon altars suggests something more consoling than the streets "running into decay" in the middle of the poem. Even the night that "clasps" the dying warriors at the beginning seems unresponsive to their sufferings, whereas the concluding lines, on one level at least, suggest that death, to the extent that it can be commemorated, need not be meaningless.

The public perspective which characterizes "Grodek" is missing

from the poem's companion piece, "Klage," which, in fact, omits
all specific reference to the war:

> Schlaf und Tod, die düstern Adler
> Umrauschen nachtlang dieses Haupt:
> Des Menschen goldnes Bildnis
> Verschlänge die eisige Woge
> Der Ewigkeit. An schaurigen Riffen
> Zerschellt der purpurne Leib
> Und es klagt die dunkle Stimme
> Über dem Meer.
> Schwester stürmischer Schwermut
> Sieh ein ängstlicher Kahn versinkt
> Unter Sternen,
> Dem schweigenden Antlitz der Nacht.

> 1 Sleep and death, the somber eagles
> 2 Resound all night around this head:
> 3 The icy wave of eternity
> 4 Would [might] swallow
> 5 Man's golden image. The purple body
> 6 Is dashed to pieces on horrible reefs
> 7 And the dark voice laments
> 8 Over the sea.
> 9 Sister of stormy melancholy
> 10 See, a fearful boat is sinking
> 11 Under stars,
> 12 [Under] the silent face of the night.
>   (I, 166)

Stylistically, "Klage" combines the short, terse lines of poems
like "Das Gewitter" with the elegiac movement of most of his
other verse. The poem's elegiac character is evident not simply
in the title and theme, but such lines as "Und es klagt die
dunkle Stimme / Über dem Meer" ("And the dark voice laments / Over the sea") epitomize Trakl's elegiac tone more
strikingly perhaps than any others in his work.

Quite in contrast to "Grodek," this poem retains the poet's
self as its point of focus rather than the anonymous warriors.
Yet "Klage" is not written in the first person, except to the
extent that the powerfully placed imperative "See" (l. 10) implies
a speaker pleading in his own name. Trakl avoids the overtly
personal by a kind of deflection: thus the self is portrayed
variously as "this head," "man's golden image," and a "fearful

boat"; yet despite—perhaps because of—this deflection, "Klage" is one of the most affectingly personal of all Trakl's poems.

Brief as it is, the poem is built out of an astonishing variety of statements and tones. The two opening lines describe a mental state in figurative terms. The following lines (3-5), which are presumably the words uttered by "sleep" and "death," provide what is probably the most all-encompassing general statement in Trakl's poetry; yet the effect of this horrendous statement is rendered characteristically ambivalent by the subjunctive form of the verb (one need only compare the uncompromising effect of the same verb—"verschlingen" ["swallow," "devour"]—in its indicative form in the last line of "Traum und Umnachtung"). The next statement (ll. 5-6) employs the old *topos* of shipwreck as a figure for the destruction of the self. In the following two lines, the tone shifts abruptly from cold, brute description to elegiac mourning. The final lines take the form of a plea to a higher being, who, as in innumerable Trakl poems, appears as a manifestation of the sister; and to the extent that the preceding lines come to seem dependent upon these concluding ones, the poem as a whole could, in fact, be described as a prayer.

Despite the variety of tones within the poem, each statement lays the groundwork for the succeeding one. The somber, sinister quality of sleep and death resounding about the head anticipates the cataclysmic icy wave; the latter image is a realization, one might say, of what was merely latent in the former. The icy wave, in turn, leads to the body shattered on the reef. The body, moreover, awakens the compassionate response of the voice over the sea, which, in turn, becomes the object of the speaker's prayer.

Yet this prayer seems curiously undemanding. The speaker asks only "See," not "Help me!" or "Save me!" The boat goes down without any indication that higher powers will ever intervene, while the stars and the night at the end remain beautiful but unresponsive. Still, the poem's bleakness is qualified by the characteristic ambivalence of attitude which runs through Trakl's work as a whole. The stars may seem unresponsive, but they are also perhaps a cosmic analogue of the precarious golden image of man. The catastrophic events of the first half of the poem—the icy wave, the shattering of the body—are answered, if not by the intervention of grace, at least by the "dark voice" of lament.

Like the brazen altars and the spiritual flame in "Grodek,"

lament is a means of preserving something of what may be destroyed. Moreover, the lament depicted in the poem is analogous to the writing of the poem itself, which, after all, is entitled "Lament." To the extent that beautiful poems can be written about destruction, something perhaps remains.

CHAPTER 6

Trakl Posthumous

FOR the first few years after Trakl's death, his distinction was more fully acknowledged than it was to be until the revival of his work during the 1950's. His death in late 1914, together with the publication of his second volume of poetry, *Sebastian im Traum,* the following year, occasioned notices in the literary sections of newspapers throughout the German-speaking countries. Both volumes were reprinted before the end of the war, and late in 1918 Trakl's publisher, Kurt Wolff, brought out a collected edition under the title *Die Dichtungen* (*The Poetic Works*).[1] Independent volumes of Trakl's poetry appeared in Czech and Rumanian translations during the first decade after his death, and individual poems can be found in a number of foreign anthologies and periodicals of that time. The influential American expatriate journal, *transition,* included the poem "Rosenkranzlieder" ("Rosary Songs"), translated by its editor Eugene Jolas, in its first issue (April, 1927), where Trakl appeared in the company of James Joyce, Gertrude Stein, and André Gide. In 1922, Paul Hindemith published musical settings of two of Trakl's finest rhymed poems, "Trompeten" ("Trumpets") and "Die junge Magd" ("The Young Maid"), and two years later Anton von Webern published his atonal settings of four free-verse poems, "Die Sonne" ("The Sun"), "Abendland" ("Occident"), "Nachts" ("At Night"), and "Gesang einer gefangenen Amsel" ("Song of a Captured Blackbird").

Yet serious and illuminating criticism of Trakl's work can scarcely be found during these years. Only Rilke's few and almost cryptic remarks, made in letters to Ludwig von Ficker and Erhard Buschbeck in 1915 and 1917, respectively, point forward to the kinds of insight which Trakl criticism was not to develop for another forty years. In these remarks, most of which I have quoted at one point or another in this study, Rilke not only recognizes the overpowering effect of Trakl's poetry on the reader but suggests a number of perspectives: the relation

136

of Trakl's literary form to the dream; the play of opposites which determines the organization of many Trakl poems; the suggestiveness of the pauses between lines; the autonomy of Trakl's poetry as a verbal universe of its own; the persistence and ambiguousness of the image of falling; and Trakl's significance in literary history in liberating the poetic image from its traditional subservience to abstract statement. All of which is only to say that Rilke, as a fellow poet working within the Symbolist tradition, had a better conceptual grasp of what he and Trakl were trying to do than did the German critics of the time.

During the following years, Trakl's name was kept alive largely through two factors: the devotion of Ludwig von Ficker and the *Brenner* circle, and the fact that by 1920 his work was seen as one of the earlier manifestations of Expressionism, which, in the years immediately following the war, had become a highly programmatic, self-conscious movement in literature and art. The major contribution of Ficker and his friends was a book, *Erinnerung an Georg Trakl* (*Remembrance of Georg Trakl*), published in 1926 on the occasion of Trakl's reburial in Innsbruck. The book gathers a number of memoirs about Trakl as well as essays concerned with his work; among other things, it reprints Karl Borromäus Heinrich's pioneering critical essay of 1913 and includes such diverse items as Trakl's letters, Ficker's account of his visit to Trakl in the Cracow hospital just before the poet's death, and an extended, though highly unreliable, biographical and critical sketch by a young Innsbruck admirer of Trakl's work, Erwin Mahrholdt, who had committed suicide even before the book appeared.

Over the years, as Trakl's poetry came to seem less and less current in the literary scene, Ficker gave away one after another of his many Trakl manuscripts to persons who wrote articles or doctoral dissertations about the poet or who otherwise showed a serious interest in his work. In the course of time, the Christian existentialist orientation which had marked *Der Brenner,* and which had made it a vital force in its earlier years, gradually became less existentialist and more Christian—indeed, Christian in a peculiarly otherworldly way. This increasingly Christian bias also came to dominate the critical approach which many of those who wrote about Trakl chose to take. One could, in fact, almost speak of an Innsbruck school of Trakl criticism—including,

besides Ficker, men such as Josef Leitgeb and Ignaz Zangerle—
whose last large monument was Eduard Lachmann's thorough-
going Christian interpretation, *Kreuz und Abend* (*Cross and
Evening*) of 1954, in which every Trakl poem is treated as a
moment within a specifically Christian drama of fall and
redemption.

Trakl's connection with the Expressionist movement could
be said to begin with the inclusion of ten of his poems in the
famous Expressionist anthology *Menschheitsdämmerung* (*Twilight of Humanity*), which appeared in 1920. Here Trakl was
associated with such other writers of his generation as Georg
Heym, Ernst Stadler, Franz Werfel, Gottfried Benn, Else Lasker-
Schüler, and August Stramm. During subsequent years, in fact,
he was almost constantly linked with Heym and Stadler, not
necessarily because of any intrinsic resemblances between them,
but because all three had died young and could thus be looked
upon as exemplifying an early phase of Expressionist poetry.
The following lines by Kurt Pinthus from his introduction to
Menschheitsdämmerung give some indication of the perspective
within which Trakl and his contemporaries came to be viewed:

All the poems in this book stem from the lament over humanity,
from the longing for humanity. Man in the absolute sense, not in his
private affairs and emotions, but humanity—that is the actual endless
theme. These poets early sensed how man sank down into twilight . . .
sank into the night of destruction ["Untergang"], only to emerge
once more in the brightening dawn of a new day. In this book, man
turns consciously from the twilight of an embracing and devouring
past and present that have been imposed upon him into the redeeming
dawn of a future which he will create for himself.[2]

In its applicability to Trakl's work, this statement contains
at best a quarter-truth. Although it employs a number of typical
Trakl terms such as "Dämmerung" (both "dawn" and "twilight"),
"Untergang" ("destruction," "decline," "going down," "setting"),
and "versinken" ("to sink down"), through its bombastic rhetoric
and, above all, its optimistic proclamation of man's coming
rebirth, it seems grossly at odds with the spirit and meaning of
Trakl's poetry.

This is not to say that it is meaningless to treat Trakl in conjunction with his Expressionist contemporaries. He certainly
knew several of the persons—for instance, Else Lasker-Schüler,
Herwarth Walden, and Oskar Kokoschka—who are generally

classified as Expressionists, and the literary and philosophical influences that helped to shape his poetry—notably Dostoevsky, Nietzsche, Hölderlin, Baudelaire, and Rimbaud—were much the same as those that stand behind many self-proclaimed members of the movement. More fundamentally, Trakl shares with Expressonism such characteristic aims as the destruction of conventional syntax and poetic diction, the stress on concrete images as the central units of poetic meaning, and the fascination with themes such as death, decay, and processes of transformation.

Yet Trakl has always fit uncomfortably within the various definitions and self-definitions of Expressionism. For one thing, unlike nearly all the writers associated with Expressionism as a movement, he was by nature a solitary figure, a writer who, moreover, lacked any programmatic sense of himself as a member of a group that could alter the course of either literature or life. Nor did he share the radical political affiliations which characterized many, though by no means all, Expressionists. Perhaps most important of all, the aggressiveness inherent in the protest and the desire for renewal voiced in such Expressionist statements as the passage by Pinthus quoted above is totally foreign to Trakl's predominantly passive and detached poetic stance.

Apart from this, the question of whether or not Trakl was an Expressionist does not seem to me to be particularly interesting today. The literary historian who employs a narrow definition of Expressionism is likely to present a limited and one-sided view of Trakl, for, because of the very context he has set up, he must seek out only those qualities which Trakl shared with his contemporaries. Perhaps because of the tendency of an earlier generation of German scholars to discuss individual poets and poems according to the "isms" to which they allegedly belong, the uniqueness and greatness of Trakl's work were consistently underestimated for many years. However, the best recent approaches to Expressionism—those, for instance, of Adolf Klarmann, Edgar Lohner, Walter Muschg, and Walter Sokel[3]—largely avoid this difficulty, for they do not only represent Trakl as a major poet, whatever his connections to Expressionism may be, but they widen the older view of Expressionism by indicating its connections with similar developments in the various arts throughout Europe and America in the 1910's and 1920's.

Perhaps because my training and reading have been centered in English and French literature as much as in German, my own

inclination is to remove the Expressionist label from Trakl
altogether and to consider his work within the mainstream of
modern literature as a whole. Throughout this study, except for
my discussion of "Das Gewitter," which shows more overtly
"Expressionist" features than most other Trakl poems, I have
steered away from the term Expressionism; instead, I have used
the terms Symbolist and post-Symbolist whenever I felt the
need to explain Trakl's work within the context of a larger
literary tradition. For these terms, to the extent that they have
come to refer to the history of modern poetry internationally,
seem far more helpful in making sense out of Trakl's poems
than does the term Expressionist, which, within literature though
not in art, suggests a specifically German context. Moreover, a
major poet often is best illuminated when he is compared to
those writers of similar stature who, even if they write in different
languages and are unaware of one another, are working within
a similar literary tradition; thus, Trakl can be linked at least
as interestingly to such other great heirs of Symbolism as T. S.
Eliot, Hart Crane, Antonio Machado, and St.-John Perse as he
can to such distinctly lesser talents in his own language as Heym
and Stadler.

Whatever the disadvantages of listing Trakl as an Expressionist,
the fact remains that until recently his reputation as a writer
was pretty much dependent on the reputation of Expressionism
as a whole. For instance, during the Nazi period Expressionism,
because of its alleged decadence and its frequently leftist political
orientation, was much in disfavor in Germany, and Trakl's work,
as a result, was largely ignored. Unlike many Expressionists,
however, he was never banned, for he was racially acceptable
and lacked clearcut political convictions, even though his distaste
for war emerges unmistakably from his poems. In the first years
after World War II, German critics gradually came to look back
on Expressionism as the last great period of their national art
and literature, and to the extent that Trakl's name was traditionally tied to the movement, his work was revived.

Although a great number of Trakl studies were published
during the 1950's, most of these already seem hopelessly dated,
at least to the degree that they allegorize Trakl's poetry in terms
of some ideological bias, be it Christian, Jungian, or existential.
One of the most influential and fascinating, though also one of
the most eccentric, of these studies, was that of the philosopher

Martin Heidegger, who presented Trakl as one of the heroes of
the modern spirit, a poet who, like Hölderlin and Rilke—on both
of whom Heidegger had written earlier—can be seen as a prophet
of the return of pure "being" ("Sein") to a coldly rationalistic
civilization.[4] Thus, for Heidegger, Trakl's "blue" imagery and
his whole concept of "Abendland" ("occident" and "evening-
land") are essentially metaphors for the realm of being. It
would seem gratuitous to complain of the wrongheadedness of
Heidegger's approach to Trakl, for Heidegger does not even
pretend to use the poets he writes about for any purpose except
the exposition of his own philosophy.[5] But Heidegger's study of
Trakl seems to me considerably less successful than his study
of Hölderlin, if only because his own philosophy is much more
akin to Hölderlin's in the first place.

During the later 1950's, Trakl studies took a significantly new
direction motivated by two developments. The first was the
recognition—initiated by four independently and almost simultaneously written studies of Trakl's debt to Rimbaud[6]—that Trakl
was working directly within the Symbolist tradition and that,
as a consequence, his poems must be viewed, at least initially,
as complex verbal structures and not, as earlier studies had
implicitly assumed, as mimetic renderings of some personal
experience, or ideology, or *Zeitgeist*. The second development
was the decade-long preparation, by Walther Killy, Hans
Szklenar, and a team of assistants, of the critical edition, which,
by the very nature of the task, necessitated the establishment
of an empirically grounded school of Trakl scholarship. To
demonstrate the interconnectedness of these developments, one
might note that Killy's study of the manuscript versions of
"Helian" served, among other things, to confirm the Symbolist
nature of Trakl's work and, in effect, to render older readings
of the poem obsolete.

A Georg Trakl literary prize, sponsored by the Austrian
Ministry of Education, has been awarded at sporadic intervals
since 1952, and its recipients have included such Trakl-influenced
poets as Christine Lavant and Christine Busta. By the 1960's
one could generally find Trakl and Kafka linked in literary
histories and encyclopedias as the two major writers within
the distinguished generation which reached maturity just before
World War I. The most telling proof of Trakl's recent fame is
the critical edition itself (finally published late in 1969), which,

with its inclusion of Trakl's innumerable and complex manuscript variants and such documents as his report cards and military passes, is, as far as I can tell, the most elaborate edition that has been devoted thus far to a twentieth-century writer in any language.

Although Trakl's critical reputation has grown steadily during the last decade, his role as a major force among practicing poets seems to have reached its peak in the 1950's. Even a superficial leafing through the individual volumes, anthologies, and journals of poetry during that period reveals a widespread influence of Trakl's tone, his peculiarities of syntax, and his characteristic vocabulary. His impact can be discerned in poets otherwise as diverse as Paul Celan, Karl Krolow, Johannes Bobrowski, Walter Höllerer, and Heinz Piontek. Take, for instance, the following poem, "Die Jahre von Dir zu Mir" ("The Years from [of] You to Me"), by Celan, one of the finest contemporary voices writing in German:

> Wieder wellt sich dein Haar, wenn ich wein. Mit dem Blau
>   deiner Augen
> deckst du den Tisch unsrer Liebe: ein Bett zwischen Sommer
>   und Herbst.
> Wir trinken, was einer gebraut, der nicht ich war, noch du,
>   noch ein dritter:
> wir schlürfen ein Leeres und Letztes.
>
> Wir sehen uns zu in den Spiegeln der Tiefsee und reichen
>   uns rascher die Speisen:
> die Nacht ist die Nacht, sie beginnt mit dem Morgen,
> sie legt mich zu dir.
>
> Again your hair is moving [waving] when I cry. With the
>   blue of your eyes
> You set the table of our love: a bed between summer and
>   autumn.
> We drink what is brewed by one who was neither myself,
>   nor you, nor a third person:
> We sip an empty and a final [thing].
>
> We watch each other in the ocean's mirrors and pass the
>   food to one another more quickly:
> night is night, it begins with morning,
> it lays me down with you.[7]

Celan's poem is Trakl-like not only in much of its imagery—
"blueness," "autumn," "drinking," "mirror," "night"—but, above
all, in the ceremonious quality achieved by its syntax and the
subtle modulations of its rhythm. The neuter noun built out of
an adjective, as in the words "ein Leeres" and "ein Letztes," is,
of course, a Trakl mannerism, though it is one which Trakl, like
Rilke, derived from Hölderlin. As in Trakl's free verse, moreover,
the pauses between the lines suggest processes and happenings
which are never directly expressed.

Yet Celan's poem is no simple imitation, but an independent
creation; it could be described as a love poem, a dialectical confrontation between self and other, such as Trakl would not have
written. Despite the breadth of reference suggested by its imagery,
the poem remains more firmly rooted in the human realm than
do Trakl's poems, which always leave the reader uncertain
whether the human or the cosmic perspective is primary. Behind
all the surface solemnity and ceremoniousness of Celan's poem
one is aware of a certain cerebral quality emanating from such
forms as the colloquial verb contraction "wein," the cliché
"schlürfen," and the conceit "setting the table of our love."
Indeed, it is this very cerebral quality which separates this
poem from Trakl's world and suggests the direction which Celan
and other poets in German were to take in subsequent years.

"Die Jahre von Dir zu Mir," printed in Celan's collection of
1952, is a relatively early poem and reflects a time when Trakl
was still a powerful and living presence for poets seeking a voice
to help them speak. During the last decade, however, precisely
when his critical reputation has continued to grow for critics
and readers, Trakl has come to seem increasingly remote to
poets. The lofty stance, the cosmic range, and the haunting
music of Trakl's poetry now mark him, with Rilke, as perhaps
the last great representative of what could be called the sublime
tradition in German, a tradition, moreover, which was the overwhelmingly dominant one within German poetry during the
last two centuries.

The antisublime, on the other hand, has always had hard
going in German. Poets who have primarily cultivated qualities
such as playfulness, wit, irony, and the refusal to be solemn have
never been accorded the status reserved for members of the
dominant tradition. Among nineteenth- and early twentieth-
century poets of the antisublime, a major figure such as Heine

has continually been underestimated and misunderstood by critics, and lesser figures such as Wilhelm Busch and Christian Morgenstern have been relegated to the categories of children's verse and light verse, respectively. The antisublime was practiced by some members of the Expressionist generation, most notably by Jakob van Hoddis, Gottfried Benn, and, somewhat later, by Bertolt Brecht,[8] but it was not until the 1960's that it has come to seem the primary vein which a large number of poets were working. Not surprisingly, contemporary poets such as Hans Magnus Enzensberger, the later Celan, and the so-called Concrete poets have often had to go to foreign literature for their models, for instance to William Carlos Williams and Robert Creeley and to the Dadaists and the French Surrealists. The only poet of distinction still showing a marked Trakl influence in the 1960's was the late Johannes Bobrowski, who, as an East German, worked outside the West German literary scene entirely.

Ironically enough, at the very time that Trakl has ceased to be a force in German poetry, his impact is being felt in the Anglo-American world. Thanks to the efforts of translators such as Michael Hamburger, Christopher Middleton, James Wright, and Robert Bly—all of them respected poets in their own right— Trakl's work has increasingly become something to reckon with for poets writing in English. The possibilities that Trakl offers are suggested in the following poem by Wright, entitled "Rain":

> It is the sinking of things.
>
> Flashlights drift over dark trees,
> Girls kneel,
> An owl's eyelids fall.
>
> The sad bones of my hands descend into a valley
> Of strange rocks.[9]

We recognize the Trakl vocabulary of "it is," "sinking," "descend," "bones," and "rocks" as well as the slow Trakl-like pauses between the various lines and stanzas, but, even more fundamentally, Trakl's example has helped Wright achieve the illusion of a direct rendering of experience, without the intrusion of the conscious mind.

In Anglo-American poetry, as opposed to German, the issue is no longer the sublime style versus the anti-sublime; the reign of the sublime, which has never had the hold on English that it has on German, was effectively destroyed through the efforts of Eliot and Pound early in this century. For poets such as Bly, Wright, Creeley, and James Dickey, the central issue is directness of vision as opposed to discursive reasoning in poetry; and in his critical pronouncements Bly, for instance, has constantly invoked Trakl as the great modern visionary poet. In one of his polemical statements he expressed Trakl's significance in these terms: "Our view of the 'modern movement' in literature is confused because we have never tried to distinguish the works which were the products of the dying tradition, like *Ulysses,* from those that came into being precisely to break the dying tradition. *Ulysses* is part of the dead world; Trakl's poems are part of the live world."[10]

For the contemporary poet in German, the "dying tradition" is the sublime tradition of Goethe, Hölderlin, Hofmannsthal, Rilke, and Trakl; quite in contrast, for the contemporary poet in English it is the ironic tradition of Eliot and Joyce. As always in the history of literature, every generation must kill its particular fathers before it can discover its particular self.

Notes and References

Chapter One

1. Werner Riemerschmid, *Trakl* (Vienna: Amandus-Verlag, 1947); Hans Mohler, *Offenbarung und Untergang: Georg Trakls galizischer Aufenthalt* (Saint Gallen, Switzerland: Tschudy, 1950).

2. *Georg Trakl: Strukturen in Persönlichkeit und Werk* (Bern: Francke, 1954).

3. Much of the biographical material in the following pages is drawn from Otto Basil's *Georg Trakl in Selbstzeugnissen und Bilddokumenten*, (Hamburg: Rowohlt, 1965). Because of the book's essentially journalistic nature I have proceeded with caution and, whenever possible, have checked the facts against other sources, especially the material included in the Killy-Szklenar edition. Basil's interviews with surviving members of the Trakl family and with Trakl's childhood friends have brought to light more material about the poet's early years than is available in any other printed source, including the critical edition. Unfortunately, Basil took many statements about the family history at face value. For the facts about Trakl's parents, including the more scandalous aspects of their life, I am indebted to the thorough researches of Johann Adam Stupp, in "Der Vater des Dichters Georg Trakl," *Süddeutsche Semesterblätter*, Nos. 17-18 (1967), pp. 31-41.

4. *Georg Trakl: Strukturen in Persönlichkeit und Werk*, p. 41.

5. "Begegnung mit Georg Trakl," in *Erinnerung an Georg Trakl: Zeugnisse und Briefe*, 2nd ed. (Salzburg: Otto Müller, 1959), p. 114.

6. Basil, p. 105.

7. Erwin Mahrholdt, "Der Mensch und Dichter Georg Trakl," in *Erinnerung an Georg Trakl*, p. 57.

8. *Ibid.*, p. 13.

9. *Ibid.*, pp. 191-92.

Chapter Two

1. For examples of some of these early influences, see my article "The Early Poems of Georg Trakl," *Germanic Review*, XXXII (1957), esp. pp. 58-60; and Reinhold Grimm, "Zur Wirkungsgeschichte Maurice Maeterlincks in der deutschsprachigen Literatur," *Revue de littérature comparée*, XXXIII (1959), 535-44.

2. See the unpublished dissertation (Washington University, 1969) by Theodore Fiedler, "Trakl and Hölderlin: A Study in Influence," pp. 64-72.

3. For more detailed statements of this structural principle, see Clemens Heselhaus, "Die Elis-Gedichte von Georg Trakl," *Deutsche Vierteljahrsschrift*, XXVIII (1954), 409-11; and my article, "The Play of Opposites in Georg Trakl's Poetry," *German Life and Letters*, N.S. XI (1958), 193-204. Throughout this book I shall use the terminology I developed in this article to describe the dichotomies— "positive" and "negative," "benign" and "malign"—out of which Trakl's poems are built. Despite the fact that Trakl, in the course of his career, developed an exceedingly subtle poetic vocabulary to mediate between opposing extremes, the poems, both in their organization and meaning, posit a framework of thought built around these extremes. I am deliberately employing what might seem an overly simple vocabulary to isolate this framework and to show how individual poems grow out of it. My critical strategy is perhaps analogous to that of those metrical analysts who, in scanning a poem, limit their categories to stressed and unstressed syllables despite their recognition that in actual fact any given syllable may be read somewhere between the extremes. In each instance the critic isolates a set of conventions which he sees governing the poem in order to show how actual poems manage to cope with these conventions.

4. For more detailed studies of Trakl's stylistic development, see, for instance, Kurt Wölfel, "Entwicklungsstufen im lyrischen Werk Georg Trakls," *Euphorion*, LII (1958), 50-81; Regine Blass, *Die Dichtung Georg Trakls: Von der Trivialsprache zum Kunstwerk* (Berlin: Erich Schmidt, 1968); and Heinz Wetzel, *Klang und Bild in den Dichtungen Georg Trakls* (Göttingen: Vandenhoeck und Ruprecht, 1968).

5. See Josef Leitgeb, "Die Trakl-Welt," *Wort im Gebirge*, III (1951), 7-39. Leitgeb's study was based on the collection *Die Dichtungen*, which contains nearly all of Trakl's mature verse. A new word count, to include the newly discovered poems and the variants in the critical edition, would be highly desirable.

6. The surviving manuscripts of the first stanza of "Die drei Teiche in Hellbrunn" contain both earlier and later revisions than this one, which, together with the manuscripts of most of Trakl's early poems, was destroyed in World War II soon after Buschbeck had published it. It is possible that Buschbeck tampered with Trakl's wording, as he is known to have done elsewhere (*see* II, 16-17). I include this revision in my discussion because, if it is faithful to Trakl's text, it represents an interesting intermediary stage between the very immature first version and the final version, which is fully in Trakl's mature style. For all the manuscripts of this stanza (the

manuscripts of the other two stanzas were destroyed), see II, 357-59.

7. *Hymnen Pilgerfahrten Algabal* (Berlin: Bondi, n.d.), p. 36.

8. The first version of the poem, entitled "Im Spital" ("In the Hospital" [I, 369]), contains a distinctly higher percentage of "positive" images than does "Menschliches Elend."

9. In Benno von Wiese, ed., *Die deutsche Lyrik* (Düsseldorf: Bagel, 1957), II, esp. 415-18.

10. The power of the line becomes even more evident when one compares it to its first version: "Die Fieberkranken packt ein helles Grausen" ("A bright terror grips the feverish" [I, 369]).

11. *Dichtungen und Schriften*, ed. Karl Ludwig Schneider and Gunter Martens (Hamburg: Ellermann, 1964), I, 208.

12. For Heym and Rimbaud, see Bernhard Blume, "Das Ertrunkene Mädchen: Rimbaud's Ophélie und die deutsche Literatur," *Germanisch-Romanische Monatsschrift*, N.S. IV (1954), esp. 113-18; for Trakl's use of this Rimbaud poem, see Reinhold Grimm, "Georg Trakls Verhältnis zu Rimbaud," *Germanisch-Romanische Monatsschrift*, N.S. IX (1959), 288-315 *passim*, as well as the interesting allusion to Ophelia in the jottings that eventually resulted in Trakl's poem "Helian" (*see* II, 449-50).

13. Compare this line with its first version, which reverts to the melodramatic manner of Trakl's early poems: "Und Fratzen gaukeln aus zerstampften Hirnen" ("And grimaces flutter out of mashed brains" [II, 92]).

Chapter Three

1. See *Erinnerung an Georg Trakl, op. cit.*, p. 116. In the recorded conversation Trakl called Whitman "pernicious" ("verderblich"), which another participant in the dialogue interpreted to mean that Whitman was too optimistic for a "thorough-going pessimist" such as Trakl.

2. My remarks on Rimbaud in this chapter were developed in more detail in my article "Georg Trakl and Rimbaud: A Study in Influence and Development," *Comparative Literature*, X (1958), 21-35. Subsequent to my article the following studies (some of which were written simultaneously with mine) appeared: Friedhelm Pamp, "Der Einfluss Rimbauds auf Georg Trakl," *Revue de littérature comparée*, XXXII (1958), 396-406; Ludwig Dietz, *Die lyrische Form Georg Trakls*, Trakl-Studien, V (Salzburg: Otto Müller, 1959), 97-101; Grimm, "Georg Trakls Verhältnis zu Rimbaud," *op. cit.*; and Bernhard Böschenstein, "Wirkungen des französischen Symbolismus auf die deutsche Lyrik der Jahrhundertwende," *Euphorion*, LVIII (1964), esp. 386-95. All of these studies, though they were initially suggested by a long-forgotten list of parallel passages of Trakl and

Rimbaud printed in Rumania a generation earlier (Adolf Menschendörfer, "Trakl und Rimbaud," *Klingsor*, II [1925], 93-96), attest to the belated recognition that the most appropriate context in which to place Trakl's mature style is neither the German lyric nor German Expressionism, as earlier scholars had thought, but rather modern European poetry in the Symbolist tradition.

3. *Briefe* (Wiesbaden: Insel, 1950), II, 71.

4. *Oeuvres complètes,* ed. Rolland de Renéville and Jules Mouquet, Pléiade ed. (Paris: Gallimard, 1951), p. 169 (my translation).

5. Rimbaud, *Leben und Dichtung,* trans. K. L. Ammer (Leipzig: Insel, 1907). References to this translation will be cited in the text.

6. See, for instance, the studies by Goffredo Stix, "Georg Trakls Helian: Eine Deutung," *Siculorum Gymnasium* (Catania, Sicily), N.S. IV (1951), 59-69; Eduard Lachmann, *Kreuz und Abend,* Trakl-Studien, I (Salzburg: Otto Müller, 1954), 78-84; and Alfred Focke, S.J., *Georg Trakl: Liebe und Tod* (Vienna: Herold, 1955), pp. 181-95. Except for Walther Killy, the coeditor of the critical edition, recent critics who have been at pains to combat the older view of Trakl's work as Christian vision or description of personal experience have had surprisingly little to say about "Helian" and have, instead, used shorter poems to make their point.

7. *In Defense of Reason,* 3rd ed. (Denver: Swallow, n.d.), pp. 40-57.

8. Reprinted in *Erinnerung an Georg Trakl,* p. 10.

9. For a far more elaborate metrical analysis of these and other lines in "Helian," see Wetzel, *Klang und Bild in den Dichtungen Georg Trakls, op. cit.,* pp. 67, 85-88. Unlike my own mode of scanning, which assumes that a poet's metrical peculiarities can be discerned simply by stressed and unstressed syllables, Wetzel's system of analysis uses four different markings—not only stressed and unstressed, but also semistressed ("unbetonte Hebung") and semiunstressed ("betonte Senkung").

10. Lachmann's Christian allegorizing is typical of Trakl's earlier commentators: "God's eyelids are 'lowered' over Helian," Lachmann writes of the final lines; "they wrap him in the blueness, the sacrifice is accepted" (*Kreuz und Abend,* p. 84).

11. See Reinhold Grimm, "Die Sonne: Bemerkungen zu einem Motiv Georg Trakls," *Deutsche Vierteljahrsschrift,* XXXV (1961), esp. pp. 237-238, for a summary of critical speculation on the name Helian. Trakl doubtless came across the name Lélian in the biographical section of the Rimbaud translation he was using (Ammer, p. 41).

12. "Briefe aus der Abgeschiedenheit: Die Erscheinung Georg Trakls," reprinted in *Erinnerung an Georg Trakl,* pp. 102-3.

13. Northrop Frye has noted the affinities of Spengler's imagery and larger intellectual framework with those of poetry: "Poets, like

critics, have generally been Spenglerians, in the sense that in poetry, as in Spengler, civilized life is frequently assimilated to the organic cycle of growth, maturity, decline, death, and rebirth in another individual form. Themes of a golden or heroic age in the past, of a millennium in the future, of the wheel of fortune in social affairs, of the *ubi sunt* elegy, of meditations over ruins, of nostalgia for a lost pastoral simplicity, of regret or exultation over the collapse of an empire, belong here [that is, among the different sets of cyclical symbols which Frye discusses]." (*Anatomy of Criticism* [Princeton: Princeton University Press, 1957], p. 160.) One could turn Frye's statement around and say simply that Spengler attempted to write history much as a poet such as Trakl wrote poetry.

14. *Op. cit.* It is noteworthy that Christian interpretations not only of "Helian" but of Trakl's work as a whole have become much less frequent since his connections with European Symbolist poetry were pointed out in the late 1950's.

15. *Erinnerung an Georg Trakl*, pp. 117-20.

16. "Entwurf des Gedichts: Über den *Helian*-Komplex," in *Über Georg Trakl* (Göttingen: Vandenhoeck und Ruprecht, 1960), pp. 52-96. My examples of Trakl's manuscript changes have been drawn from Killy's discussion both in this essay and in another which appeared in the same book, "Perspektiven des Gedichts," pp. 38-51. Since the critical edition presents slightly different readings, the citations in my text are to the critical edition alone.

Chapter Four

1. The absence of a comma after "blutet" indicates that this verb may be read either as transitive or intransitive. If transitive, the object is "Legenden," in which case the imperative "Lass" would not take the same object, but could be read to mean something like "No more."

2. Northrop Frye has described the displacement of the idyllic from the "upper" to the "lower" world as a central aspect of English Romantic imagery (*see* "The Drunken Boat: The Revolutionary Element in Romanticism," *Romanticism Reconsidered*, ed. Frye [New York: Columbia University Press, 1963], pp. 1-25).

3. Heselhaus, "Die Elis-Gedichte von Georg Trakl," *op. cit.*, pp. 386-89, and J. Stinchcombe, "Trakl's 'Elis' Poems and E. T. A. Hoffmann's 'Die Bergwerke zu Falun'," *Modern Language Review*, LIX (1964), 609-15.

4. See Frye, *Fearful Symmetry: A Study of William Blake* (Princeton: Princeton University Press, 1947), pp. 49-50; and "The Drunken Boat," *op. cit.*, for examples of the transformations which this imagery undergoes in English Romantic and modern poetry.

Wolfgang Preisendanz has convincingly shown that many of Trakl's idyllic images—for instance, the shepherd and his flock, the blackbird, the grove, the small boat, and the colors silver and purple—can be traced back to such minor late eighteenth-century hymnic poets as Matthisson, Voss, Salis-Seewis, and Stolberg (*see* "Auflösung und Verdinglichung in den Gedichten Georg Trakls," *Immanente Aesthetik/ Aesthetische Reflexion* [Munich: Fink, 1966], esp. pp. 255-60.) Neither the underground nature of Trakl's idyllic imagery nor its high degree of stylization can, however, be found in these German poets.

5. All the surviving manuscripts of the poems are actually typescripts with Trakl's handwritten corrections. Thus, we do not have evidence for all the stages of their composition, as we do for a number of Trakl poems. The first surviving version of the "Elis" poems is an early draft of the first of the two sections of the poem entitled "Elis." The second version contains "An den Knaben Elis" (in its final version), followed by an early version of the two sections of "Elis" (*see* I, 372-75; and II, 146-48).

6. The allusions to Hoffmann and Hofmannsthal were pointed out in the article by Stinchcombe, *op. cit.*, pp. 611, 614-15; the Rimbaud allusions, in my article "Georg Trakl and Rimbaud," *op. cit.*, p. 32; the biblical allusions, by Lachmann in *Kreuz und Abend, op. cit.*, p. 93. Preisendanz traces the olive tree and the boat to Matthisson and Stolberg respectively ("Auflösung und Verdinglichung," pp. 255-57), but these images appear so frequently in Trakl that one cannot speak of an influence from these poets specifically on "Elis." I shall describe the Nietzsche allusion in more detail here since I have not seen it mentioned by earlier commentators. The passage in *Zarathustra* reads as follows:

> Gold sah ich in deinem Nacht/Auge blinken,—mein
> *Herz* stand still vor dieser Wollust:
> —*einen goldenen Kahn* sah ich blinken auf nächtigen
> Gewässern, einen sinkenden, trinkenden, wieder winkenden
> *goldenen Schaukel-Kahn!*

> I saw gold gleaming
> in your night-eye,—my heart stood still with delight
> [sensual pleasure]:
> —I saw a gold boat gleaming on nocturnal waters, a
> sinking, drinking, gold rocking-boat that gleams again.

(*Also sprach Zarathustra*, III, "Das andere Tanzlied," 1, in Nietzsche, *Werke*, ed. Karl Schlechta [Darmstadt: Wissenschaftliche Buchgesellschaft, 1966], II, 470—italics mine.)

Trakl's lines, "Ein goldener Kahn/ Schaukelt, Elis, dein Herz am einsamen Himmel," echo the phrase "einen goldenen Kahn" and the words "Herz" and "Schaukel-Kahn" from Nietzsche's passage. In addition, Nietzsche's words "Auge," "Gold," "Nacht," "sinken," and "trinken" all appear in the two "Elis" poems.

7. *Sämtliche Werke*, ed. F. Beissner (Stuttgart: Kohlhammer, 1951), II, 117.

8. See Leitgeb, "Die Trakl-Welt," *op. cit.*, p. 34.

9. *Ibid.*, p. 14. As I have indicated earlier, Leitgeb's word count has been rendered obsolete by the critical edition.

10. Jost Hermand looks at the "Elis" poems as a reworking of Hölderlin's myth of history in "Der Knabe Elis: Zum Problem der Existenzstufen bei Georg Trakl," *Monatshefte*, LI (1959), 225-36. For a searching critique of Hermand's article and an approach to Trakl's poetry as "negative parody" of Hölderlin's myth of history, see Theodore Fiedler, "Trakl and Hölderlin," *op. cit.*, pp. 113-43.

11. *Sämtliche Werke*, II, 663-64.

12. Frye's seminal study, cited earlier, is *Fearful Symmetry*. For some authoritative statements by the Beissner "school," see Beissner, *Hölderlin: Reden und Aufsätze* (Weimar: Böhlau, 1961); Lawrence F. Ryan, *Hölderlins Lehre vom Wechsel der Töne* (Stuttgart: Kohlhammer, 1960); and Ulrich Gaier, *Der gesetzliche Kalkül: Hölderlins Dichtungslehre* (Tübingen: Niemeyer, 1962).

13. The distinction I draw between Rimbaud's and Hölderlin's influence is perhaps too absolute, for Hölderlin was to exercise a considerable, if not decisive, influence on Trakl's syntax and imagery. For a thorough study of the influence of Hölderlin's stylistic mannerisms on the later Trakl, see Fiedler, "Trakl and Hölderlin," pp. 149-80.

14. *Ibid.*, pp. 104-7.

15. See Mahrholdt's essay in *Erinnerung an Georg Trakl, op. cit.*, p. 35.

16. *Manshape that Shone: An Interpretation of Trakl* (Oxford: Blackwell, 1964), pp. 11-12 and *passim*.

Chapter Five

1. Hanns Haeckel, "Verfall und Verfallenheit—Anlässlich eines Deutungsversuchs an einem Gedicht Georg Trakls," *Zeitschrift für deutsche Philologie*, LXXVIII (1959), 369-94.

2. Lachmann, *Kreuz und Abend, op. cit.*, pp. 55-56, 216-32.

3. *Erinnerung an Georg Trakl, op. cit.*, p. 10.

4. *Collected Poems: 1909-1935* (New York: Harcourt, Brace, 1936), p. 94.

5. See Fiedler, "Trakl and Hölderlin," *op. cit.*, pp. 155-66.

6. The early study is that of Mahrholdt in *Erinnerung an Georg*

Trakl (*see* pp. 31, 32, 36, 39, 41, 53, 77, 81-82). The recent study
is Basil, *Georg Trakl in Selbstzeugnissen und Bilddokumenten, op.
cit.* (*see* pp. 15, 16, 18, 25, 29-30, 32, 33, 72, 88). It goes without
saying that a poem so firmly grounded in the Symbolist tradition
as "Traum und Umnachtung" has only the most limited usefulness
as a biographical source. How much reliable data can the biographer,
after all, collect from such supposedly "personal" poems as Yeats's
"The Tower," Eliot's "Ash Wednesday," or Rimbaud's *Une Saison
en Enfer?*

7. Trakl's phrase "ein wildes Tier" (II) probably echoes Rimbaud's "bête féroce," rendered as "wildes Tier" in Ammer's translation (p. 182).

8. See my chapter "The Possibility of a Long Poem" in *On Wordsworth's 'Prelude'* (Princeton: Princeton University Press, 1963), pp.
99-129, for a development of this notion about the Symbolist "long"
poem. I did not include Trakl in this discussion because he was still
so little known in the Anglo-American world at the time.

9. The idea that Trakl's work is more relevant as a whole than as
a collection of individual poems is represented most powerfully,
though for different reasons, by Martin Heidegger and Walther Killy.
Heidegger's statement in his Trakl essay, "Every great poet com-
poses only out of a single poem" ("Jeder grosse Dichter dichtet nur
aus einem einzigen Gedicht," in "Georg Trakl: Eine Erörterung seines
Gedichtes," *Merkur,* VII [1953], 26), is less specifically a comment
on Trakl himself than on Heidegger's own esthetics. Killy, working
within a traditional literary-historical context, maintains this
point of view as a result of his discovery, while working on the critical
edition, that Trakl often interchanged images and lines without regard
to the poem they were originally meant for (*see Über Georg Trakl,
op. cit.,* p. 26, and my discussion in Chapter 3). On the other hand,
critics who write studies of individual poems, through the very nature
of their enterprise, usually insist on the autonomy (and distinction)
of the poem itself. For example, Emil Staiger, after a detailed reading
of "Der Spaziergang" ("The Promenade" [I, 44-45]), concludes by
praising Trakl as a master of the short lyric: "When people once
again dare to profess happiness and serenity, Trakl will still speak to
them as one of the greatest German poets, as the creator of
"Verklärter Herbst" ["Transfigured Autumn" (I, 37)], "Ein Winterabend," "Seele des Lebens" ["Soul of Life" (I, 36)], and many
other small creations . . ." ("Zu einem Gedicht Georg Trakls,"
Euphorion, LV [1961], 296). In turn, the very organization of this
book has caused me to argue for the autonomy of individual poems,
though I could well imagine writing a different type of book which
stresses less the shape of particular poems than Trakl's strategies in
using language to cope with an otherwise unbearable reality. By the

same token, my preoccupation with "Helian" and "Traum und Umnachtung" while thinking out the present book has convinced me more than ever not only of the greatness of these two poems but also of Trakl's mastery of the longer form.

10. Ideally I should like to have included a full discussion of "Offenbarung und Untergang" in the present study. Somewhat shorter than "Traum und Umnachtung" and smaller in scope (it is centered less on the family than on the brother-sister relationship), "Offenbarung und Untergang" is more cryptic in its language and less rooted in an identifiably "real" world, yet, unlike the earlier poem, it follows a discernible line of narrative development in the form of a penitential journey. A full discussion would have to take into account its close relationship to an extraordinary untitled dramatic fragment (I, 455-59) which Trakl wrote about the same time.

11. The other six poems, all written between May and early July, are "Das Herz" ("The Heart" [I, 154-55]), "Der Schlaf" ("Sleep" [I, 156]), "Der Abend" ("Evening" [I, 159]), "Die Nacht" ("Night" [I, 160]), "Die Schwermut" ("Melancholy" [I, 161]), and "Die Heimkehr" ("Homecoming" [I, 162]).

12. For a somewhat different approach to the language and imagery of "Das Gewitter," see Heselhaus' perceptive reading in *Deutsche Lyrik der Moderne von Nietzsche bis Yvan Goll* (Düsseldorf: Bagel, 1962), pp. 230-36.

13. It is possible that Else Lasker-Schüler, whom Trakl met in March, 1914, and to whom he dedicated "Abendland," influenced the new style.

14. *Erinnerung an Georg Trakl*, p. 190.

15. Despite the lack of particularity, "Grodek," together with "Im Osten" ("At the Eastern Front" [I, 165]), was included in an anthology of German World War I poetry issued during the Nazi period (*Deutsche Dichtung im Weltkrieg*, ed. Ernst Volkmann [Leipzig: Phillip Reclam, 1934]).

16. See Basil, *Georg Trakl in Selbstzeugnissen und Bilddokumenten*, p. 76.

Chapter Six

1. For the corrected dating of this edition, see Ludwig Dietz, "Zur Druck- und Textgeschichte der Dichtungen Georg Trakls," *Jahrbuch der deutschen Schillergesellschaft*, VI (1962), esp. 349-52.

2. *Menschheitsdämmerung* (Hamburg: Rowohlt, 1959), p. 25.

3. Klarmann, "Expressionism in German Literature: A Retrospect of a Half Century," *Modern Language Quarterly*, XXVI (1965), 62-92; Lohner, "Die Lyrik des Expressionismus," *Expressionismus als Literatur: Gesammelte Studien*, ed. Wolfgang Rothe (Bern: Francke,

1969), pp. 107-26; Muschg, *Von Trakl zu Brecht: Dichter des Expressionismus* (Munich: Piper, 1961); and Sokel, *The Writer in Extremis: Expressionism in Twentieth Century German Literature* (Stanford: Stanford University Press, 1959).

4. Heidegger, "Georg Trakl: Eine Erörterung seines Gedichtes," *op. cit.*, pp. 226-58.

5. For an attack on Heidegger's study of Trakl, see W. H. Rey, "Heidegger-Trakl: Einstimmiges Zwiegespräch," *Deutsche Vierteljahrsschrift*, XXX (1956), 89-136.

6. All are listed in the footnotes to Chapter 3.

7. *Mohn und Gedächtnis* (Stuttgart: Deutsche Verlagsanstalt, 1952), p. 28.

8. Trakl, I might add, had his own antisublime moments. For instance, the critical edition prints the following self-parody of the "It is . . ." style of "Psalm" and "De Profundis":

> Es ist ein Hurenhaus in das ein besoffener Dichter fällt
> Es ist ein grauer Eckstein, von Hunden verbrunzt
> Es ist ein Furtz dessen Duft unsere Nasen umweht . . .

> It is a whorehouse into which a drunk poet falls
> It is a gray curbstone, stained by dogs' semen
> It is a fart whose scent blows about our noses.

(II, 126)

What separates Trakl above all from poets of the antisublime is that it would never have occurred to him (or to Ludwig von Ficker, for that matter) to publish lines such as these. For an interesting statement on the gap separating Trakl from contemporary German youth, see Preisendanz, "Auflösung und Verdinglichung in den Gedichten Georg Trakls," *op. cit.*, pp. 261, 488-89.

9. *The Branch Will Not Break* (Middletown: Wesleyan University Press, 1963), p. 52. For a statement about Trakl's impact on Wright, see Robert Bly, "The Work of James Wright," *The Sixties*, No. 8 (1966), pp. 59-62.

10. *Ibid.*, p. 4.

Selected Bibliography

PRIMARY SOURCES

1. In German

Gedichte (Leipzig: Kurt Wolff, 1913).

Sebastian im Traum (Leipzig: Kurt Wolff, 1915).

Die Dichtungen, ed. Karl Röck (Leipzig: Kurt Wolff, 1918). First collected edition of his mature poems.

Erinnerung an Georg Trakl (Innsbruck: Brenner, 1926). First collection of letters as well as miscellaneous criticism.

Aus goldenem Kelch, ed. Erhard Buschbeck (Salzburg: Otto Müller, 1939). First publication of early writings.

Dichtungen und Briefe, ed. Walther Killy and Hans Szklenar. Two volumes (Salzburg: Otto Müller, 1969). The definitive critical edition.

2. In English

Twenty Poems of Georg Trakl, tr. James Wright and Robert Bly (Madison, Minn.: The Sixties Press, 1961).

Selected Poems, ed. Christopher Middleton and tr. Robert Grenier, Michael Hamburger, David Luke, and C. Middleton (London: Cape, 1968). Largest selection in English.

SECONDARY SOURCES

Despite the fact that Trakl's stature as a major poet has been acknowledged for a relatively short time, the amount of secondary literature on him is quite large, if only because of the many doctorates which German universities have produced over the years. The first Trakl dissertation goes back to 1926 (Ernst Bayerthal, "Georg Trakls Lyrik: Analytische Untersuchung," University of Frankfort), but neither it nor the majority of dissertations written on Trakl since that time have anything of consequence to tell the reader today. Indeed the total number of bibliographical items containing useful factual information and/or good criticism is disappointingly small. The following bibliography includes not only what seems to me the best Trakl scholarship but also those writings which, despite my own

157

disagreements with them, have been sufficiently influential or provocative to interest the modern reader:

BARTH, EMIL. *Georg Trakl* (Krefeld: Scherpe, 1948). A distinguished early appreciative essay.

BASIL, OTTO. *Georg Trakl in Selbstzeugnissen und Bilddokumenten,* Rowohlt Monograph 106 (Hamburg: Rowohlt, 1965). The fullest biographical account, though marred by its journalistic method.

BÖSCHENSTEIN, BERNHARD. "Wirkungen des französischen Symbolismus auf die deutsche Lyrik der Jahrhundertwende," *Euphorion,* LVIII (1964), 375-95. Survey of French influence.

BRINKMANN, RICHARD. *Expressionismus: Forschungsprobleme 1952-1960* (Stuttgart: Metzler, 1961), pp. 30-42, 83-87. A review of research.

BROWN, RUSSELL E. "Time of Day in Early Expressionist Poetry," *PMLA,* LXXXIV (1969), 20-28. Through the analysis of a single motif, indicates the distance between Trakl and his Expressionist contemporaries.

CASEY, T. J. *Manshape that Shone: An Interpretation of Trakl* (Oxford: Blackwell, 1964). An attempt to define the meaning of Trakl's images through a study of the contexts in which they occur.

CIERPKA, HELGA. "Interpretationstypen der Trakl-Literatur: Eine kritische Betrachtung der wissenschaftlichen Arbeiten über das Werk Georg Trakls" (Free University of Berlin dissertation, 1963). A detailed critique of the various, often conflicting approaches which have been applied to Trakl.

DIETZ, LUDWIG. *Die lyrische Form Georg Trakls,* Trakl-Studien V (Salzburg: Otto Müller, 1959). A study of Trakl's formal devices and the literary traditions to which they belong.

————. "Zur Druck- und Textgeschichte der Dichtungen Georg Trakls," *Jahrbuch der deutschen Schillergesellschaft,* VI (1962), 340-52. Clears up some long-standing errors on the dates of and circumstances surrounding early Trakl editions.

Erinnerung an Georg Trakl (Innsbruck: Brenner, 1926). Contains such useful materials as Heinrich's pioneering critical essay of 1913, Limbach's record of a Trakl conversation, and some of Rilke's remarks on Trakl.

FICKER, LUDWIG VON. *Denkzettel und Danksagungen,* ed. Franz Seyr (Munich: Kösel, 1967). Collects some of Ficker's various writings about Trakl and Trakl scholarship.

FIEDLER, THEODORE. "Trakl and Hölderlin: A Study in Influence" (Washington University dissertation, 1969). Builds on the various studies of Rimbaud's influence to show that Hölderlin was less crucial than Rimbaud in Trakl's development.

GEORGE, EMERY E. "On Seeing and Hearing the Poem: An Experiment with Trakl's 'Afra'," *Orbis Litterarum*, XXI (1966), 202-21. A linguist's reading of a poem.

GRIMM, REINHOLD. "Georg Trakls Verhältnis zu Rimbaud," *Germanisch-Romanische Monatsschrift*, N.S. IX (1959), 288-315. The most exhaustive of the various studies of Rimbaud's influence.

————. "Zur Wirkungsgeschichte Maurice Maeterlincks in der deutschsprachigen Literatur," *Revue de littérature comparée*, XXXIII (1959), 535-44. Extends the method of the preceding study to the influence of Maeterlinck on the early Trakl.

————. "Die Sonne: Bemerkungen zu einem Motiv Georg Trakls," *Deutsche Vierteljahrsschrift*, XXXV (1961), 224-46. An elaborate thematic study relating Trakl to earlier literary traditions.

GRÖBENSCHÜTZ, EDITH. "Zur Datierung im Werk Georg Trakls: Im Zusammenhang mit einem kürzlich bekanntgewordenen Brief," *Euphorion*, LVIII (1964), 411-27. A detailed account of the problems in dating a single letter and a related poem.

HAECKEL, HANNS. "Verfall und Verfallenheit: Anlässlich eines Deutungsversuchs an einem Gedicht Georg Trakls," *Zeitschrift für deutsche Philologie*, LXXVIII (1959), 369-94. An anti-modernist's attack on one Trakl poem and, by implication, on the whole Symbolist tradition.

HAMBURGER, MICHAEL. *Reason and Energy: Studies in German Literature* (London: Routledge and Kegan Paul, 1957), pp. 239-71. The book which succeeded in introducing Trakl, as well as other writers in German, to the Anglo-American world of letters.

HEIDEGGER, MARTIN. "Georg Trakl: Eine Erörterung seines Gedichtes," *Merkur*, VII (1953), 226-58. Criticism as unashamedly personal vision, with all the triumphs and pitfalls that go with this approach.

HESELHAUS, CLEMENS. "Die Elis-Gedichte von Georg Trakl," *Deutsche Vierteljahrsschrift*, XXVIII (1954), 384-413. A pioneering study that not only explicates the "Elis" poems but sets up the essential framework which subsequent Trakl criticism was to follow.

————. "Gesang des Abgeschiedenen," *Die deutsche Lyrik: Form und Geschichte*, ed. Benno von Wiese (Düsseldorf: A. Bagel, 1957), II, 401-8. Good close reading.

————. *Deutsche Lyrik der Moderne von Nietzsche bis Yvan Goll* (Düsseldorf: A. Bagel, 1962), pp. 228-57. A sensitive study of Trakl's use of imagery and its relation to that of other modern poets in German.

HÖLLERER, WALTER. "Trübsinn" and "Grodek," Die deutsche Lyrik:
Form und Geschichte, ed. Benno von Wiese (Düsseldorf: A.
Bagel, 1957), II, 409-24. Good close readings.

KEMPER, HANS-GEORG. Georg Trakls Entwürfe (Tübingen: Niemeyer,
1970). An approach by way of the manuscript materials in the
critical edition.

KILLY, WALTHER. Wandlungen des lyrischen Bildes (Göttingen:
Vandenhoek und Ruprecht, 1956), pp. 116-35. Places Trakl
within the history of German poetic imagery.

————. Über Georg Trakl (Göttingen: Vandenhoek und Ruprecht,
1960). Essays in which the coeditor of the critical edition announces and analyzes some of his more startling findings.

————. "Die Entstehung von Trakls 'Melancholie'," Wort in der
Zeit, X (1964), 14-20. Study of the development of a poem
through various manuscript versions.

LACHMANN, EDUARD. Kreuz und Abend: Eine Interpretation der
Dichtungen Georg Trakls, Trakl-Studien I (Salzburg: Otto
Müller, 1954). Exasperating, but still the best of the many
Christian interpretations.

LEITGEB, JOSEF. "Die Trakl-Welt," Wort im Gebirge, III (1951),
7-39. Contains useful word counts, though out of date since the
appearance of the critical edition.

LINDENBERGER, HERBERT. "The Early Poems of Georg Trakl,"
Germanic Review, XXXII (1957), 45-61. A pedestrian effort but
contains some information that goes beyond the treatment of the
early work in this book.

————."The Play of Opposites in Georg Trakl's Poetry," German
Life and Letters, N.S. XI (1958), 193-204. An early, only
partially successful attempt to work out what was to become
the conceptual framework behind this book.

————. "Georg Trakl and Rimbaud: A Study in Influence and
Development," Comparative Literature, X (1958), 21-35. An
ambitious attempt to redirect the course of Trakl criticism by
indicating the Symbolist nature of his work.

MAGNUSON, KARL. "Consonant Repetition in the Lyric of Georg
Trakl," Germanic Review, XXXVII (1962), 263-81. An analysis
of sound patterns, with both the strengths and limitations inherent
in this critical genre.

MUSCHG, WALTER. Von Trakl zu Brecht: Dichter des Expressionismus
(Munich: Piper, 1961). A brilliant, controversial attempt to
define Trakl's place in modern German literature and to argue
for his status as a major writer.

NEUMANN, ERICH. Der schöpferische Mensch (Zurich: Rhein, 1959),
pp. 247-310. A Jungian interpretation by a distinguished mind.

PRAWER, SIEGBERT. "Grammetrical Reflections on Trakl's 'De Profundis'," *German Life and Letters,* N.S. XXII (1968), 48-59. Uses a close reading of one poem to suggest Trakl's relation to modern poetry as a whole.

PREISENDANZ, WOLFGANG. "Auflösung und Verdinglichung in den Gedichten Georg Trakls," *Immanente Ästhetik/Ästhetische Reflexion,* ed. W. Iser (Munich: Fink, 1966), pp. 227-61, 485-94. Brilliant study of Trakl's approach to poetic language and his reworking of earlier German poetic traditions.

REY, W. H. "Heidegger-Trakl: Einstimmiges Zwiegespräch," *Deutsche Vierteljahrsschrift,* XXX (1956), 89-136. A searching, hardhitting attack on Heidegger from the standpoint of the literary historian.

RITZER, WALTER. *Trakl-Bibliographie,* Trakl-Studien III (Salzburg: Otto Müller, 1956). An indispensable bibliography which badly needs bringing up to date.

SCHNEIDER, KARL LUDWIG. *Der bildhafte Ausdruck in den Dichtungen Georg Heyms, Georg Trakls und Ernst Stadlers: Studien zum lyrischen Sprachstil des deutschen Expressionismus* (Heidelberg: Winter, 1954). A formal analysis of imagery which indicates Trakl's relationship to two Expressionist contemporaries.

—————. *Zerbrochene Formen: Wort und Bild im Expressionismus* (Hamburg: Hoffmann und Campe, 1967). Includes remarks on Trakl's relationship to tendencies and figures in modern art and literature.

SOKEL, WALTER. *The Writer in Extremis: Expressionism in Twentieth-Century German Literature* (Stanford: Stanford, 1959), pp. 49-50, 72-78. Relates Trakl to German Expressionism and to modernism as a whole.

SPOERRI, THEODOR. *Georg Trakl: Strukturen in Persönlichkeit und Werk* (Bern: Francke, 1954). A psychiatric study that is more successful with the personality than the work.

STAIGER, EMIL. "Zu einem Gedicht Georg Trakls," *Euphorion,* LX (1961) 279-96. A genteel close reading by an old master of the art.

STUPP, JOHANN ADAM. "Der Vater des Dichters Georg Trakl," *Süddeutsche Semesterblätter,* Nos. 17-18 (1967), 31-41. As a result of meticulous researching, uncovers illuminating new information about Trakl's family background.

SZKLENAR, HANS. "Ein vorläufiger Bericht über den Nachlass Georg Trakls," *Euphorion,* LIV (1960), 295-311. An early report out of the workshop of the critical edition.

—————. "Beiträge zur Chronologie und Anordnung von Georg Trakls Gedichten auf Grund des Nachlasses von Karl Röck," *Euphorion,*

LX (1966), 222-62. Explains some central problems in organizing the critical edition; includes excerpts from Röck's diary describing Trakl's day-to-day presence among his Innsbruck friends.

WALTER, JÜRGEN. " 'Orientierung auf der formalen Ebene'—Paul Klee und Georg Trakl: Versuch einer Analogie," *Deutsche Vierteljahrsschrift*, XLII (1968), 637-61. Suggestive and generally successful comparison of a Klee watercolor with a section of "Helian."

WETZEL, HEINZ. *Klang und Bild in den Dichtungen Georg Trakls*, Palaestra 248 (Göttingen: Vandenhoek und Ruprecht, 1968). The most comprehensive study of Trakl's metrics and use of sound patterns.

WÖLFEL, KURT. "Entwicklungssufen im lyrischen Werk Georg Trakls," *Euphorion*, LII (1958), 50-81. The first attempt to indicate precisely the stages of Trakl's development as a poet.

Index

163